EASTERN HEROES
BRUCE LEE SPECIAL VOL.2 #5

EDITORIAL

Welcome to the Bruce Lee Special Vol. 2 No. 5.

In this issue, we delve into the enduring legacy of Bruce Lee and the ripple effects of his untimely death. As film companies scrambled to capitalise on the martial arts craze he ignited, the search was on for a new star who could match Lee's electrifying on-screen presence and unparalleled fighting skills. When no one could rise to the challenge, the industry turned to the next best thing: creating Bruce Lee look-alike clones.

Brian Bankston takes us on a fascinating journey through this phenomenon in his article "*IMITATING THE DRAGON: The Historical Significance of Bruceploitation Cinema,*" exploring the cultural and historical impact of these imitators.

For collectors, Mike Nesbitt offers an in-depth review of the "Enter the Clones" box set, a must-have for any Bruce Lee enthusiast. We also feature an exclusive interview with Frank Djeng, who discusses the Bruce Lee USA Tour, providing unique insights into Lee's influence across America.

Additionally, Simon Pritchard covers the European premiere of "Enter the Clones," while Jason McNeil delves into the world of Bruce Lee comic strips.

All this and much more await you in this packed edition. Enjoy the journey as we celebrate and examine the legend of Bruce Lee!

Rick Baker

CONTENTS

- 4. Imitating The Dragon
- 36. Bruceploitation film reviews
- 52. Collecting Bruce Lee LPs
- 67. Enter the Clones: USA Tour
- 77. The Resurgence of Bruceploitation
- 80. Legend Of The Paper Dragon
- 85. Bruce Lee Photo Gallery
- 112. The Yellow Jump Suit
- 116. Dream, Believe, Achieve

CONTRIBUTORS

- Mike Nesbitt – UK
- Johnny Burnett – Scotland
- Frank Djeng – USA
- J.T. Williams – USA
- Brian Bankston – USA
- Jason McNeil – USA

Special Thanks
David Gregory - Severin Films - USA

Editor In Chief - Rick Baker
Design & Layout - Tim Hollingsworth
Front Cover Artwork - Russell Fox

Imitating The Dragon

The historical significance of Bruceploitation Cinema
By Brian Bankston

In the fifty years since his death, Bruce Lee (Li Jun Fan; Li Siu Lung) remains the most influential and important martial arts figure of all time. For a man who only made four completed motion pictures in his adult years, his staying power is remarkable. His short 32 years on Earth made him legendary and an almost mystical figure that is talked about just as much today as he was back in the 1970s when the name 'Bruce Lee' was literally everywhere all around the world.

This article—the most complete of its kind in English—takes a look at the progression of this oft-maligned sub-genre known as Bruceploitation: movies that in one form or another--existed to make money off Bruce Lee's name and flamboyant personality. Most were cash-grabs; few were respectful to the material; some were parodies made in good fun; and a great many were wild excursions into tasteless entertainment. This exploitation of the Little Dragon wasn't limited to these cheaply made movies, but also used in the advertising of them; and every market around the world participated in it.

But first, we go back to the time before Lee died. This sub-genre went through a gradual evolution before its primary Hong Kong-based phase between the years 1976-1978. In the beginning, there were actors and films that were being promoted as a new Bruce Lee, or those that imitated Lee before the actual Bruce Clone movement began; there were even examples of treacherous film producers attempting to secretly profit from Lee at the height of his popularity while he was still alive.

These early, pre-clone movies adopted the trend of having similarities in the film's Chinese titles. This followed in the tracks of what the Italian westerns had done in the wake of the Leone-Eastwood movies by having 'Dollars' somewhere in the name. Selected box-office numbers are included where applicable so as to put the film's into context with their local appeal. Once we're knee-deep into the cloning stage, there's coverage of two of the major Lee impersonators; followed by a short list of other important actors, related individuals and examples of some of the trashiest movies this lowbrow sub-genre has to offer.

In Hong Kong, Bruce Lee achieved god-like status and was summarily worshiped as one upon his return to the then British colony in the summer of 1971. His Hollywood career wasn't taking off the way he wanted; so things took an upturn when Lo Wei's wife at the time, Liu Liang Hua, lured him into a lucrative deal (for Hong Kong) to make films for the struggling Golden Harvest, a new independent company founded by Raymond Chow, Leonard Ho, and director Huang Feng.

History would be made when he began filming two movies for director Lo Wei, *THE BIG BOSS* (1971) and *FIST OF FURY* (1972). Neither movie was anything that hadn't already been seen before, but Lee's domestic popularity from *THE GREEN HORNET* and his onscreen charisma struck a chord with local audiences. *THE BIG BOSS* smashed box office records in HK with a 23-day haul of HK$3,197,416.

For a HK movie in those days, a poor to average showing ranged between 3-6 days in theaters; 7-14 days was generally a million grosser or more; but 20+ days was unheard of. Naturally, the Bruce imitations that followed used key elements from his movies. His TV appearances weren't off limits, either.

Bruce Lee had already made a name for himself in the United States playing Kato in *THE GREEN HORNET* and other appearances on American television shows. At the same time, he was making fast friends with Hollywood's finest. Citizens of Hong Kong treated him like a hometown hero upon his return, celebrating his breach of the American market and loving him for turning his attention to making movies for local audiences.

Lee would break box office records again with his second movie directed by Lo Wei, *FIST OF FURY* in 1972. It surpassed *THE BIG BOSS's* big numbers, making HK$4,431,424 in 29 days of theatrical release. Lee, the King of Kung Fu, would now be even more meticulous and decisive than he already was. His high standards meant he would have to continuously top himself. Lee was a complicated man. He was also arrogant and had a short fuse. With Lee, it was a constant climb to the top; even if he'd already reached it. If his next film made less than FIST, it would be a step backward in his eyes.

However, Bruce Lee had an extraordinary level of confidence. He knew his capabilities and that he held sway over the audience to a degree never before achieved by another actor. To the paying audience, he was a god. Magazine articles in HK at the time regularly reiterated that Lee was not a god, but a man like any other. It was an unusual magnitude of hero worship comparable to Mexico's adoration for wrestling sensation and actor El Santo, The Saint in English.

As for Bruce, he'd made a prediction to the media that his next movie would make HK$5 million at the local box office. Remarkably, and just as Lee had predicted, his directorial debut, *WAY OF THE DRAGON*, hit the unprecedented HK$5 million mark--surpassing it with a total of HK$5,307,350. Critics weren't exactly enthusiastic about his first time directing, pointing out how Bruce's WAY lacked finesse even if the action was his usual top tier showcase.

Even before his success in Hong Kong, Bruce was obsessed with being a leading man in Hollywood; as much as his unhealthy preoccupation with his body and how he looked on camera. In one example not long before his death in 1972, he had the sweat glands removed from his armpits because he felt it soiled his appearance on-camera. Doing so carries with it life-changing risks to an assortment of bodily and nervous system functions.

His long-desired lead status in a US co-production came in the form of 1973s ENTER THE DRAGON. Lee reportedly came up with the title--his self-recognition for penetrating the international market as a Chinese leading man in a non-Chinese production. His dream would come true, but he wouldn't live long enough to see it.

THE EXPLOITATION OF BRUCE LEE

In America and Hong Kong, Lee had many friends; one of the closest was childhood pal Unicorn Chan. An acrobat and stuntman, his friendship with Lee was covertly used to make money off the superstar's name in a movie titled *FIST OF UNICORN* (1973). In the fall of 1972, Shing Hai Films (Star Sea Motion Pictures) took out a full page ad promoting Lee's

participation. It's unclear who or how many were involved in the deception, but Bruce offered to design the fights for his friend's big break in front of the camera so long as it was understood he would not be appearing with him. While Bruce worked on the set, one or more individuals shot footage of Lee choreographing the action with the intention of using it in the movie in some way. When Lee found out, he reportedly threatened a lawsuit if his presence wasn't removed. He was featured prominently in the HK trailer, shown working on the set. It was Unicorn Chan's debut in front of the camera, but the publicity was largely focused around Lee.

This likewise didn't stop overseas distributors from trying to make bank off Lee's name when the film played in America in 1973 as BRUCE LEE AND I (not to be confused with the Betty Ting Pei produced biopic from 1976).

A small company called Pacific Grove initially made up posters for the movie boasting, "The most exciting Kung Fu picture ever directed by Bruce Lee". At the bottom stating, "Directed by and choreographed by Bruce Lee". The company even used a still photo of Bruce working with Unicorn Chan on the set as its main image (see insert image). An alternate version was also issued using an image from the movie and removed wording declaring Bruce Lee as the director; although the movie itself displays Bruce Lee as the film's director and fight designer. Additionally, the dubbed version retains the deceptive Bruce Lee footage as well as images of him that are awkwardly spread throughout the film.

This early instance of Bruceploitation foreshadows the prime ingredients the sub-genre would use a few years later. The films were frequently about the movie industry and the duplicitous figures in front and behind the camera. In the case of FIST OF UNICORN, the exploiting of Lee was occurring right in front of him. Had he lived, this eternally-scorned sub-genre would never have existed.

The earliest example of exploiting the Dragon posthumously occurred a few months after he died, and came from Raymond Chow and directed by a former AD at Shaw Brothers named Wu Shih. 1973s BRUCE LEE: THE MAN AND THE LEGEND (released in America in a re-edited version in 1984) was akin to a Mondo movie opening and ending with Lee's funerals in HK and in Seattle, Washington. In between, a narrator describes lots of footage of Asian and American film stars talking about Lee while odd musical cues play on the soundtrack. The emphasis

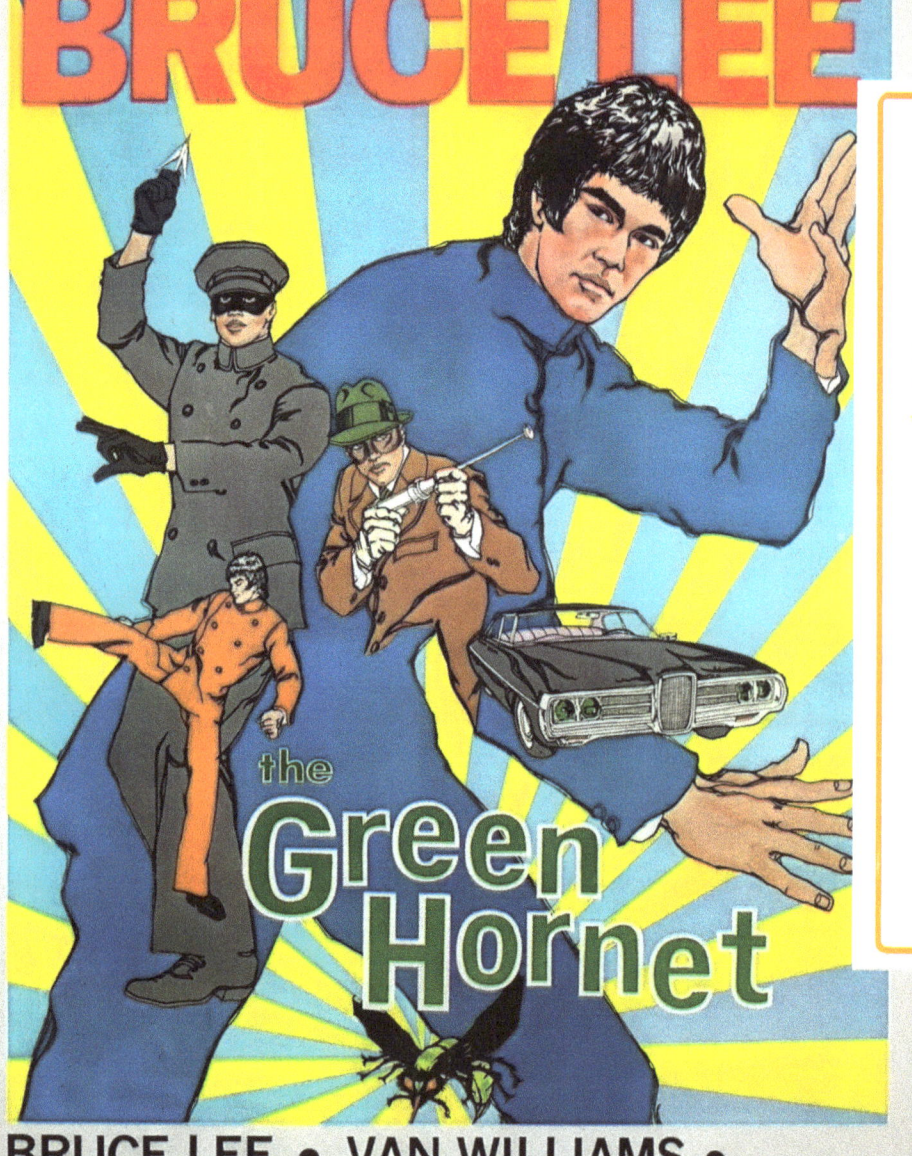

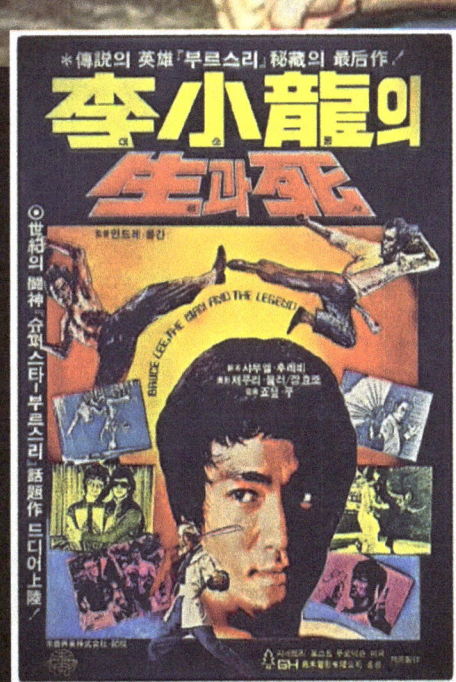

on the man's life and death, married to the clips of his funeral, would form the crux of so many of the imitator movies that would slowly begin seeping into theaters between 1974-1975 and picking up steam by 1976, the Year of the Dragon.

Not to be outdone by devious Hong Kong filmmakers, American producers decided to stitch four episodes of the old GREEN HORNET (1966-1968) television series together and release it to theaters in 1974 as a new Bruce Lee movie. Titled THE GREEN HORNET, it made enough money to prompt producer Laurence Joachim to poach more footage from the series. This second go-round, though, was marketed like a Bruce clone picture with the title FURY OF THE DRAGON (1976).

Putting aside the avarice involved in bleeding profit from a dead man's name, these two unethical productions have eye-catching comic book poster artwork, the second of which is by Philip Williams. He painted around two dozen Kung Fu movie posters in both Europe and America--some of the titles include STREET GANGS OF HONG KONG (1973), aka THE DELINQUENT, THE CHINATOWN KID (1977), and Italian posters for THE WAY OF THE DRAGON (1972), THE CHINESE BOXER (1970), and THE CHIVALROUS KNIGHT (1973), aka CHINESE GODFATHER.

Before there were actors performing literal impersonations of Bruce Lee, Taiwanese Kung Fu pictures had actors implementing Lee's on-screen mannerisms into their performances. In some cases, producers were seemingly lifting ideas Lee was utilizing in his then unfinished GAME OF DEATH; a movie he began shooting in 1972, but wouldn't see the light of a film projector till 1978 when it was completed and released.

DRAGON FROM TAIWAN

In 1972, Taiwan needed their own Bruce Lee, so Taiwanese martial arts instructor Tong Lung (aka Luo Chen, the elder brother of Alexander Luo Rei) was being promoted as The Little Dragon's match. The media had been doing the same with Chen Kuan Tai at Shaw Brothers when BOXER FROM SHANTUNG (1972) grossed over HK$2 million. Chen was also a martial arts teacher and tournament champion. Tong Lung, though, had a physique that was not only comparable to Lee's, but was even more muscular. Tong's first movie was the HK-Taiwan co-production, THE FEROCIOUS BROTHERS (1972). The film's Chinese title translates to 'The Dragon and Tiger Cross the River'. The Chinese title of Bruce Lee's WAY OF THE DRAGON is 'The Fierce Dragon Crosses the River'. With Taiwan marketing its own action movie

star as comparable to Bruce Lee, they would also give him the stage name of Tong Lung; which happened to be the name of Lee's character in WAY OF THE DRAGON.

What else is notable about the Chinese name for THE FEROCIOUS BROTHERS is that it's also a reference to Jimmy Wang Yu's blockbusting trendsetter THE CHINESE BOXER (1970), known in Chinese as 'The Dragon and Tiger Meet'. For this occasion, combining two hit films names (CHINESE BOXER's HK$2+ million and WAY's HK$5+ million) would hopefully equal to big box office. Similarities in these film's Chinese titles are one of the steps in the evolution of this peculiar Bruce Clone phenomenon.

Tong's other early 70s movies bore similarities to the Chinese titles of Lee's films as well. In some cases, the same applied to the English-translated titles, too. THE GROWLING TIGER's (1974) Chinese title is 'Tiger Killer From Tangshan'. This is a play on Lee's THE BIG BOSS (1971), which is known as 'Big Brother From Tangshan' in Chinese. In another example of title manipulation, Tong Lung's ON THE VERGE OF DEATH (1973) was released in some markets as BRUCE LEE VS. CHINESE FRANKENSTEIN.

Just as Wang Yu's directing debut inspired numerous 'Hard Fist & Kick' movies using 'Dragon' and 'Tiger' in the title, the wildly successful Bruce Lee pictures did the same by influencing other filmmakers to mimic them in the hopes it would produce a sizable hit. Independent companies were especially hungry for a BIG BOSS-sized smash that would hopefully make the producers lots of money; and enable a fledgling company to survive in an industry cranking out 110-130 movies a year.

In Europe, THE GROWLING TIGER either had the name 'Bruce Lee' in the title, or the poster artwork depicted Tong brandishing nunchucks to give audiences the impression they're getting some Lee-like action. In Germany it was called REVENGE FOR BRUCE LEE while in America it was known as THE BLACK DRAGON VS. THE YELLOW TIGER (see above insert). The film's Chinese poster featured as its primary selling point, Tong Lung battling a black martial arts fighter; likely influenced by the ballyhoo of Bruce Lee battling Kareem Abdul Jabbar in the footage filmed for GAME OF DEATH in 1972.

When Bruce began shooting GAME OF DEATH in late '72, he wanted to top himself yet again. He was consumed by thoughts of giving audiences something new in every film he made. For GAME, he envisioned a plethora of martial artists battling inside a multi-level pagoda that was possibly inspired by the one constructed specially for Chang Cheh's HAVE SWORD WILL TRAVEL (1970). One of those fighters was 7'2" basketball player Kareem Abdul-Jabbar. His casting was integral to the promotion of Lee's film; while also being crucial to the metamorphosis of Bruce Imitator cinema.

Once Warner Bros. offered Lee the lead in what would become ENTER THE DRAGON (a co-production with Golden Harvest and Lee's own company, Concorde Pictures), he put GAME OF DEATH on hold till he realized his dream to be a leading actor in a non-Chinese movie. And then, a month before ENTER THE DRAGON hit American theaters, Bruce Lee died.

CHINESE CONNECTIONS: BRUCE AND BETTY

On July 20th, 1973, a week before ENTER THE DRAGON was shown in HK theaters, Bruce Lee passed away in the apartment of actress Betty Ting Pei, a woman who was also his mistress. Media reports at the time were alight with accusations and conspiracy theories that branded responsibility for Lee's death on everything and everybody but Lee himself. Ting Pei was blamed, Raymond Chow was blamed; conspiracies abounded that Lee was poisoned by the Triads, he was a victim of the Death Touch, and so on. Lee had only been a superstar for a few short years and the public perceived him as something of a Superman; to say his sudden death shocked the masses is an understatement. Some who couldn't come to grips with the fact the man had died even believed Lee had faked his own death. It's a fascinating topic that, in some ways, remains shrouded in mystery 50 years later.

On the record, his death is listed as cerebral edema, swelling of the brain. To this day, there are only theories on how it happened. In light of recently surfaced letters between Lee and Bob Baker (who played the Russian fighter in FIST OF FURY), it's possible Lee's drug addiction contributed to his death. You can't push your body past its limitations while ingesting harmful drugs like cocaine and LSD and not expect your body to give out at some point. Lee loved himself some marijuana too; but coupled with harder drugs and a fast-living lifestyle, his penchant for pushing his body far more than resting it was a recipe for disaster. His short time on Earth only fueled wild imaginations and it wasn't

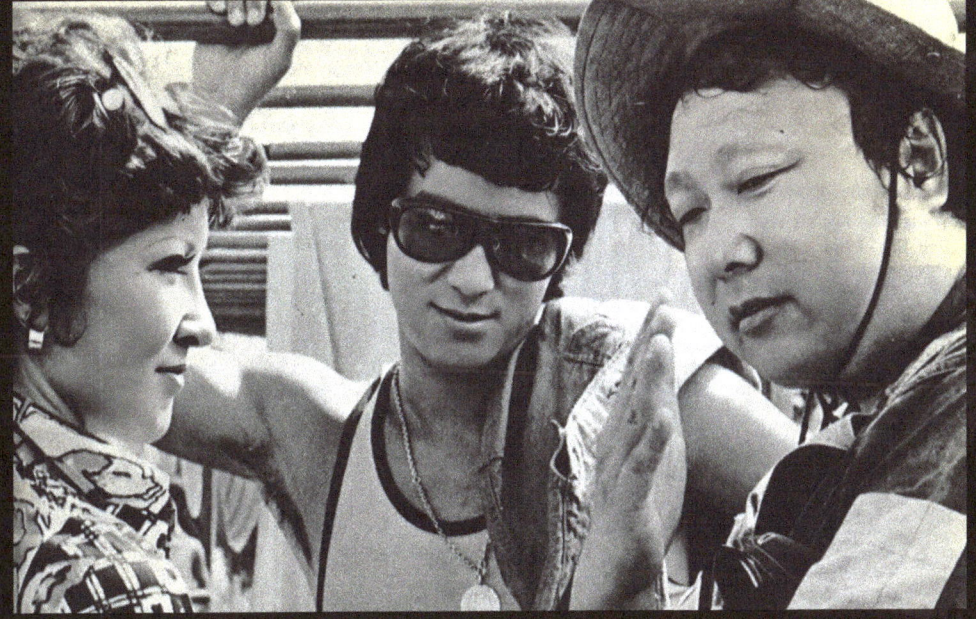

long before salacious movies about his life would be made... and thus the next, and highly controversial, level in the evolutionary chain of the Bruce Clone phase would begin.

By 1976, the sub-genre would be in full swing; spearheaded by *BRUCE LEE AND I*, a biopic produced in 1975 by Betty Ting Pei, filmed at Shaw Studio, and distributed by them. In the early months of 1973, it was reported that Run Run Shaw had agreed to pay Bruce Lee HK$2.5 million (US$400,000) to star in an historical actioner to have been directed by Chu Yuan. Filming was estimated to have begun in April of 1973. Since that production never got off the ground due to the death of the star, this serious-minded biopic was the next best thing. Till legalities were settled, Bruce Lee's name was listed only as "The Superstar". Danny Lee (Li Hsueh Hsin) was playing the charismatic Kung Fu master. There was another film coming out with a similar Ting Pei-centric storyline called *GOLDEN SUN*. That picture featured actress Chen Pei Ling playing Betty Ting Pei.

Danny Lee stated in an interview at the time he wasn't pleased with his work on *BRUCE LEE AND I* because he wasn't given a copy of the script beforehand; all of his direction was given to him by director Lo Mar everyday he reported to the set. However, he did an incredibly good job in the role.

This one was unique in that it was told from the perspective of the last person to see Lee alive, that being his lover, Betty Ting Pei-- the lead role in the movie. Curiously, this example of Bruceploitation is possibly the most respectable and accurate depiction of this time in the man's life. That's not saying a great deal, but important events are treated more tactfully than they were in other films dealing with the subject matter. *BRUCE LEE AND I* made HK$644,908 in its 7 days of theatrical play. In America it was released as *BRUCE LEE: HIS LAST DAYS, HIS LAST NIGHTS* and had additional nudity not found in the HK cut. Despite being slickly directed by award-winning director John Lo Mar-- who was known for helming dramas prior to this--the picture did nothing to salvage Ting Pei's reputation.

Considering what was going on during this time period and the public's and media's seething hatred towards Ting Pei, this production is one of the most important in the Bruce imitator series. Several other Bruce-biopic films would feature actresses playing Ting Pei with varying degrees of fact vs. fiction. Prior to Danny Lee, there had already been a few films starring a man who got his first leading role playing Bruce Lee.

ENTER THE IMITATORS

When the Bruce clone sub-genre reached its final stage, those movies shared commonality with Lee's outer-body obsession by focusing on recapturing his looks, his attire, his mannerisms, his life... but tossing out his style of action choreography. Having been spoiled on Hollywood methods, Lee wasn't interested in traditional Chinese-style action design. His style was somewhere in the middle. It was superior to American action sequences but lacked the more complicated move sets seen in innumerable Hong Kong Kung Fu pictures.

After his death, Chinese movie-makers ignored Lee's preference for limited kicks and punches and went for the longer fighting sequences. Lee was a perfectionist, picking and choosing his scripts wisely, and avoided shooting more than one film at the time. When he died, Chinese filmmakers would mass-produce imitator movies; including the ones that either put "Bruce Lee" in a pseudo-biographical adventure, or created an entirely new one that exploited his name and appearance.

In some cases, these movies would use archival footage of Bruce while he was alive and even footage from his funeral that would end up as a plot point.

Taiwanese born Ho Tsung Tao (or Ho Chung Tao) was the first, and arguably the most famous of the Bruce imitators since his movies were both regularly promoted and screened in HK and Taiwan. He was the most successful, and certainly the most well known, of the three major actors to do these kinds of movies; the other two being

Ho Chung-Tao (Bruce Li)
Counter Attack
龍的影子
aka
The Chinese Stuntman

Bruce Le and Dragon Lee. Phonetically we pronounce the name Bruce Li as Bruce "Lie", but it is actually pronounced as "Lee". In old HK magazines, Bruce Lee was almost always written as "Bruce Li", which is the same pronunciation as Lee.

As with most of the Chinese KF stars, Ho Chung Tao got into lots of fights when he was a boy; only it was him being bullied. Growing up a fat kid, Ho got into physical education and studied various martial arts like Karate, Judo and Western-style boxing. When he got out of school he became a bit player in martial arts films. In those days, Ho was extremely poor. To his parents disapproval, he wanted to be an actor and continued pursuing his desire to become a star despite the struggle. According to Ho in an interview, during one three-month period he never had more than a dime in his pocket. When he got into movies in 1972, he was making HK$6 a day. His parents continued to try and convince him to learn a trade for more reliable income but the stubborn young man stuck it out.

His first time playing in a lead role came in 1972 with CONSPIRACY. The film wasn't completed and released till sometime in 1975. In America it was christened ENTER THE PANTHER to try and associate itself with Bruce Lee mania. Ho was paid HK$2,000 for his part (approximately US$350). The hard times would get a little easier by 1974.

He got his first lead as Bruce Lee in SUPER DRAGON (1974)--a movie known in America as THE DRAGON DIES HARD and also BRUCE LEE, A DRAGON STORY. SUPER DRAGON was an amateurish start to this sub-genre and uniformly poor in all departments. Its box office take was certainly below average at HK$418,372 for six days in theaters. It must've made more money in Taiwan, Singapore or some other Southeast Asian market because more similar films were coming.

Allied Artists released it at the height of the American Kung Fu boom as THE DRAGON DIES HARD in 1974. Unfortunately, it was films like this that killed the legitimacy of Hong Kong and Taiwanese-made martial arts films in English-speaking markets. Major studio interest had all but evaporated by 1975, giving the road to a slew of smaller outfits that made tidy profits off these pictures of both high and low quality.

If SUPER DRAGON was never sold anywhere outside of Southeast Asia there possibly would never have been as many of these films that came after it, if any at

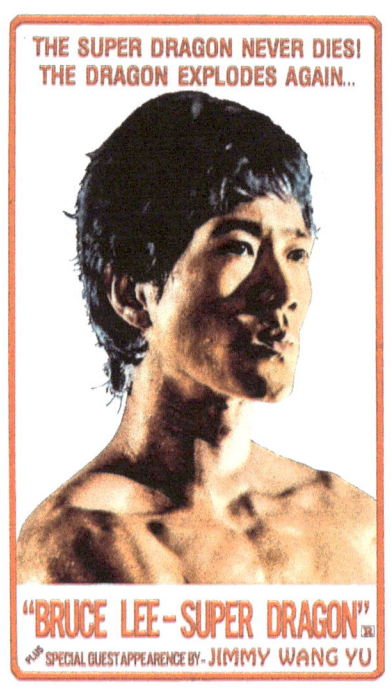

all. The films got more salacious and the advertising even more outrageous. The global interest in Kung Fu movies let Chinese film producers know that their style of action picture would remain a hot seller on the export market; and internationally, people wanted more Bruce Lee, even if the man himself was dead.

Ho Chung Tao was reportedly unaware that his name was being changed to Bruce Li for SUPER DRAGON. He stated in 1978 he was very angry upon seeing the film with his name credited as "Bruce Li" instead of "Ho Chung Tao as Bruce Lee". Producers encouraged him to continue being a pretend Lee so he reluctantly went along.

The most bizarre of the Bruce Li pictures, and residing on the wacky end of the Bruce Clone spectrum, was BRUCE LEE AGAINST SUPERMEN (1975). This is easily the most ridiculous movie on Ho Chung Tao's resume next to his dueling with a Kung Fu Gorilla in BRUCE LEE, THE INVINCIBLE (1978)--a movie that has nothing to do with Lee other than its exploitative title. There's layers of Bruce-isms on display: Ho is billed again as Bruce Li; he also plays Kato and a character named Carter; and there's the obligatory mimicking of Lee's mannerisms while trying to rescue a scientist who has discovered a formula to turn petroleum into food. And then Bruce battles Superman... only it's not George Reeves but Lung Fei in black tights and a white cape. If that weren't enough, there's nudity and a sex scene.

Presumably, this movie was partly inspired by Shaw's production of SUPERMEN VS

Atlas International and Robert Chow present a Yu - Yun Production »Goodbye Bruce Lee - his last Game of Death«
Directed by: Lin Pin and Harold B. Swartz
Music: Arpad Bondy
with: Lee Roy Lung, Ronald Brown, »Big« Jonny Floyd, Mun Ping
Produced by: R. Chow and Chang Lung
World distribution Atlas International, Munich
Technicolor/Scope

Pei, the filmmakers, and the actors that continued making them as "maggots" and "scum". There was definitely endearment by some towards Bruce Li, though.

THE NEW GAME OF DEATH was the first of the imitations to utilize motifs from Bruce Lee's postponed GAME OF DEATH film he began in 1972. An independent feature, it was picked up for distribution and released by Shaw Brothers Studio around the time they'd finished filming BRUCE LEE AND I in October of 1975. This film made even less money than SUPER DRAGON, only amassing HK$164,249 in six days of release. That didn't stop it from being snatched up and released all over the world. Most markets utilized the GOODBYE, BRUCE LEE: HIS LAST GAME OF DEATH title.

In America, Aquarius Releasing re-edited the film, adding an interview with Kareem Abdul Jabbar, and then saddled the movie with the title GOODBYE, BRUCE LEE: HIS LAST GAME OF DEATH. The US poster is naturally as confusing as it is deceptive; as unscrupulous movie distributors tended to be back in the 1970s. In the case of this movie, legal action was taken against at least some Pennsylvania theaters showing it due to outrage from irate customers who paid to see Bruce Lee on the screen. Theaters were ordered to remove all misleading advertisements and potentially provide restitution to customers who felt cheated by the posters. Deception and greed are a universal language, and a dialect spoken by all industry showmen around the world.

THE ORIENT (1974); the first of their official co-productions with foreign companies. Bruce Li wears similar super-attire that Lo Lieh, Shih Szu and their Italian co-stars don in the Shaw picture; only these red tights are emblazoned with the Green Hornet insignia.

By the time Bruce Li made the more serious CHINESE CHIEH CHUAN KUNG FU (TANG SHAN JEET KUNE DO in Chinese) in 1976, he was able to use his real name of Ho Chung Tao. Unfortunately for Ho, some foreign territories advertised the picture as starring the actual Bruce Lee. Adding to the confusion, the movie was also known as BRUCE LEE SUPER DRAGON (see above), BRUCE LEE SUPERSTAR and LEGEND OF BRUCE LEE. Additionally, this was the fourth time the actor would collaborate with martial arts colleagues Lung Fei and Shan Mao (who was murdered in 1977) in the ongoing series of Lee-alike movies.

HK audiences were largely ambivalent towards these films. Critics and journalists were mostly hostile towards them--calling them tasteless and even referring to Ting

With two Bruce bombs on the domestic front, Chinese producers went a different route for Bruce Li's next interpretation of the dead superstar. Titled GOLDEN SUN (1975), it would be better known under its more descriptive moniker of BRUCE LEE, WE MISS YOU. It would also be released

Bruce Lee Special Vol.2 No.5 15

in Asian territories as 18 FORMS OF JEET KUNE DO and in Great Britain as THE DRAGON DIES HARD (not to be confused with SUPER DRAGON released in America under the same title). This time, Bruce Li plays three roles: Bruce's ghost, Bruce in flashback, and a martial arts student trying to find out who killed him. Directed by Li Kuan Chang (director of 1973s WAY OF THE TIGER starring Tong Lung, who was discussed earlier), the film is highlighted by an impressive fight on top of a moving bus; something you didn't see very often in those days.

BRUCE LEE, WE MISS YOU was similar in ways to Ting Pei's BRUCE LEE AND I, but a tabloid version of those events, inferring Bruce was killed by the mob and aided by Ting Pei. It probably didn't help quell the rumors that the Triads had killed Bruce since Betty--who allegedly attempted suicide in 1972 (although she and her family denied this) due to Lee's refusal to leave his wife for her--entered into a relationship with Triad figurehead and actor Charles Heung in 1976. Heung was allegedly married at the time he and Betty began seeing one another, so she once again found herself embroiled in another scandal that only fueled more questions about Lee's death and the citizenry's hatred of her.

On the Chinese Zodiac, 1976 was the Year of the Dragon. It was also a Bruce Boom for Ho Chung Tao. Multiple movies about Lee's life were being shot--from various point of views and with varying degrees of success. One movie in particular directed by Wang Hsing Lei (director of Tan Tao Liang's first movie, 1973s HERO OF THE WATERFRONT) was marketed as "bringing an authentic Bruce Lee story to the screen"; that film being HE'S A LEGEND, HE'S A HERO, the English title of JEET KUNE DO. The promise of authenticity couldn't entice HK patrons since the film made a barely average HK$499,066 in 7 days of release.

In America, though, HE'S A LEGEND, HE'S A HERO was shortened to the more exploitable moniker, THE DRAGON LIVES. Director Wang was the indy scenes equivalent to Shaw's director, the revered Cheng Kang, in that he took upwards of a year to make a movie. This was indy company First Film's sole attempt at imitating Bruce Lee. It should also be mentioned that the Chinese are notoriously superstitious, so any promotion of authenticity for a film about an incredibly famous actor who died under mysterious circumstances extends to what the people believed to be true at the time.

Another Bruce Li flick released in 1976 was *BRUCE LEE'S SECRET* (Wing Chun Jeet Kune Do in Chinese), a film that was also released in Chinese-speaking territories as *THE STORY OF THE DRAGON* among many other alternate titles. Known in America as *BRUCE LEE'S DEADLY KUNG FU*, it co-starred Carter Wong (Huang Chia Tah) and told of Lee's days in San Francisco. The film had two directors, Chen Hua and Chang Si Hui (William Chang Kee, director of *CALAMITY OF SNAKES* infamy), taking their first time at bat. The former was previously a DP for Ng See Yuen. The latter was a camera assistant for Chang Cheh and later for Ng See Yuen as well. He is also the son of filmmaker Lan Tien Hong, a name that will come up again later on.

Allegedly, *BRUCE LEE'S SECRET* was accepted into the Milan Film Festival. Much like these films were made with foreign markets in mind, the picture played in several Western theater lines in Asian territories. The local box office was no clone of the real Lee's Golden Harvest successes, though--making a paltry HK$252,474 in an unusually long theatrical run of 14 days for such low earnings.

EXIT THE DRAGON, ENTER THE TIGER (known in HK as *BRUCE LEE: THE STAR OF ALL STARS*), directed by fan favorite Lee Tso Nam, was closer in tone to *BRUCE LEE, WE MISS YOU*, alias *GOLDEN SUN*. Bruce Li was again playing multiple roles--as both Bruce Lee and a friend of the MA superstar. In this one, Bruce tells his friend, "If I die, find out why". The Betty Ting Pei character (called Suzie Yang here) is written differently from the *BRUCE LEE, WE MISS YOU* movie. Ironically, Lee's now widely known drug use is discussed in this film, but written as if it were only a rumor.

Lee Tso Nam's movie is superior to Li Kuan Chang's WE MISS YOU picture. The opening title of the US release is imaginatively done as the title 'Exit the Dragon' retreats to the background as 'Enter the Tiger' comes into the foreground. The English dubbing, however, is among the worst of the genre. Still, for an indy release, the movie made money in America and could've been titled 'Exit the Pocket, Enter the Cash Register'. Its success meant non-Oriental producers would be unleashing more fake Lee in theaters.

Meanwhile, Hong Kong producers were more than covering their costs from the licensing fees so they would continue making them. The Anglo markets were the primary target for these films, and they would become more prevalent once Bruce Le and Dragon Lee entered the impersonator fray.

Filming at the same time as *BRUCE LEE: THE STAR OF ALL STARS* was *FIST OF FURY PART 2* (1977), considered one of the best movies of its kind. Both films starred Bruce Li, both directed by Lee Tso Nam, and both made for Jimmy Shaw's production company, Hong Kong Alpha (Seven Seas Motion Pictures). The latter picture would likely have never been made had it not been for Lo Wei getting drunk on his birthday and blurting out his plans to sequelize his own

FIST OF FURY to his guileful friend and presumed confidant, Jimmy Shaw Shao Feng. This wacky story was written about for the first time in English in THE WILD, WILD EAST: DUEL OF THE INDEPENDENT FILM COMPANIES PART 5 which you can read at Cool Ass Cinema.com. The following abbreviated version is largely additional information not included in the above article.

It's an extremely complicated story that would've made a great Kung Fu Comedy if shot as it happened. As funny as the details are, this key example of unprincipled film producers led to much animosity and ruined relationships. The divorce of Lo Wei and his first wife Liu Liang Hua, followed by Raymond Chow siding with Lady Liu to not give her ex-husband the rights to FIST OF FURY, was already the start of a wildfire. But when Jimmy Shaw Feng stole Lo's idea, it likewise caused a quake between him and Lo's new wife, Hsu Li Hwa. Jimmy Shaw was allegedly romantically involved with Lady Hsu's sister, so this was viewed as a betrayal. Shaw (no relation to the movie mogul brothers) tried to reverse the ordeal by explaining in an interview that he persuaded Lo Wei to fast-track his movie but took the idea for his own when Lo didn't move fast enough to his liking. Shaw Feng went on to state Hsu Li Hwa had previously borrowed money from him and this was her way of inadvertently paying back a debt.

The short version is Lo Wei was unable to shoot his own script as written, so he had to rewrite it and rename it NEW FIST OF FURY. An ambitious stuntman and martial arts choreographer named Jackie Chan was being promoted to lead actor status (for the second of three career jump-starts) in what would be a string of bombs for the increasingly frustrated Lo Wei. NEW FIST was not a promising start to a career that would unexpectedly explode two years later.

Once Chan became a big star in 1978, devious film producers pulled similar stunts that so many in HK, Taiwan, and overseas had done with the Lee-alike movies. After THE FEARLESS HYENA (1979) brought in HK$5 million, producer Li Lang Guan saw dollar signs and dusted off his Shun Li Film Company's old Chan flick from 1973 titled CUB TIGER FROM KWANG TUNG (1973). He hired actor-turned-director Chin Hsin to shoot new footage with Simon Yuen Siu Tien and Korean thunder-kicker Kwan Young Moon to try and make both a new flick and a fast buck at the box office. This mess of a movie was called MASTER WITH CRACKED FINGERS (1979). In

Spanish-speaking markets, *MASTER WITH CRACKED FINGERS* was promoted as *LA FURIA DE JACKY* (*THE FURY OF JACKY, or JACKIE* in some instances). Lobby cards for this film used stills from *NEW FIST OF FURY* while listing Jackie (as Chen Lung) and Yuen Siu Tien as the stars and Chin Hsin as director. Some of the posters used imagery from the US promotion of Chan's *THE BIG BRAWL* (1980).

Going back to the two dueling *FIST OF FURY* sequels, they had just as much action going on behind the scenes as in front of it. The publicity surrounding the battling film producers was so great, another, yet unnamed Taiwanese movie producer intended to shoot his own *FIST OF FURY* film. It's unknown if this particular movie got made, or if it became *FIST OF FURY III* that began filming in 1978 and emerged in 1979 bearing the original title of *JEET KUNE THE CLAWS AND THE SUPREME KUNG FU* (*JEET KUNE EAGLE CLAW* in Chinese). This film also starred Ho Chung Tao once more playing Chen Zhen, the character he played in *FIST OF FURY 2* (1977); and the same character Bruce Lee famously portrayed in the 1972 original.

With 1976 being the Year of the Dragon, Chinese film producers probably saw it as a sign of good luck to make sequels to Lee's breakout successes; so many more flicks of fury were coming.

Possibly the best of these films was *BRUCE LEE: TRUE STORY*, known here as *BRUCE LEE: THE MAN, THE MYTH* (1976). It was certainly one of the very few that were hits in Hong Kong. Taiwan may have yielded better box office for some of these films, but most were rejected domestically. Like *BRUCE LEE AND I* (1976), *THE MAN, THE MYTH* took the subject seriously as directed by Seasonal founder Ng See Yuen.

However, no matter how polished the latter title was, audiences simply weren't going to forgive Ting Pei anytime soon. Likely due to the mature approach to the material, *THE MAN, THE MYTH* was well received by HK audiences. It had a 13-day run and amassed HK$1,282,742. If you were to be curious about this peculiar style of MA film, this motion picture would be a great place to start. In this case, starting at the top and working your way down is preferable.

By 1978, Ho Chung Tao had tired of playing Bruce Lee. His entire career had been built around imitating a dead man and he was beyond ready to be himself on-screen. Unfortunately, he had fewer opportunities to do so as a new superstar named Jackie Chan exploded onto the scene that same

year. Ho Chung Tao did briefly find himself among the top ten most popular actors in 1978. DYNAMO (1978) wasn't a Bruce clone picture, but it had Ho Chung Tao wearing that yellow jumpsuit from GAME OF DEATH. It was a mostly bland, but tenuously entertaining behind the scenes look at an actor being made and manipulated by an advertising agency. HK audiences took to the story, making the movie HK$1,338,539. It spent 9 days in theaters.

What was saddening about Ho's career was that even when he starred in a movie where he was playing anyone but Bruce Lee, the marketing would find a way to keep the connection between Ho and the late film star. One such picture was 1979s BLIND FIST OF BRUCE directed by Kam Bo for his Kam Bo Motion Pictures. The Chinese title, BLIND FISTS GHOST HAND, bore no affiliation with Bruce Lee. This was also one of the many deceptive independent KF flicks that took advantage of elder Yuen Siu Tien's surprise popularity after the two hit indy Jackie Chan pictures for Seasonal Corporation.

If labeling BLIND FIST with 'Bruce' in the title for export wasn't enough of a blow to Ho Chung Tao, other non-Lee films he did like THE CHINESE STUNTMAN (1981) were marketed in some foreign territories with both Bruce Lee and Jackie Chan on the poster! In Germany, the film was called BRUCE LEE THE UNDEFEATED. Overseas, Ho was still being marketed as Bruce Li, so he was going to be saddled with the Lee-alike brand no matter how far away he got from the Bruce mannerisms.

Another example was the trashy BRUCE LI IN NEW GUINEA (1979). Like BLIND FIST OF BRUCE, BRUCE LEE THE INVINCIBLE and CHINESE STUNTMAN, Ho Chung Tao doesn't even play a character named Bruce, but the Chinese distributors felt the need to use "Bruce Li" in the English export title to sell it overseas. In some areas, the film was called BRUCE LEE IN SNAKE ISLAND and even THE BIG BOSS IN BORNEO.

But where Ho Chung Tao was never comfortable playing an imitation of Bruce Lee, there was another man who seemed to wholeheartedly embrace it in those days.

MY NAME CALLED BRUCE LE

Easily the most flamboyant and enterprising of the Bruce's is Huang Chien Lung (Huang Kin Lung). Bruce Li may be the most respectable of the Bruce doubles, but the most prolific on the international scene was Bruce Le. Where Bruce Li wasn't keen on playing Bruce Lee, Bruce Le wore those roles like a badge of honor. And there was a clear distinction in the quality of both men's work. Where Ho Chung Tao's movies told a story and were, for the most part, reasonably well made, Huang's films lacked cohesion with barely any plot to speak of. Oftentimes looking like they made it up as they went along, the patchwork style of Le's flicks and the plethora of alternate titles only added to the rampant incoherence in every aspect of the productions.

A discovery of director Wang Feng (Wong Fung), Burma-born Huang Chien Lung (a few years before he'd take the name of Bruce Le) was a real martial artist who ran a Kung Fu school in Macau. He'd began his MA training in both Chinese and Japanese arts at the age of 11 and later became just as hungry for the film business as he was for martial arts. Huang signed with Shaw Brothers in 1973 after accepting Wang Feng's invitation to appear in RIVALS OF KUNG FU, a story about famous Chinese martial arts hero Wong Fei Hung. Huang made six movies at Shaw Brothers, the most famous of which was THE SUPER INFRAMAN (1975); a motion picture where he had no opportunity to show much skill as a KF actor.

Reportedly, at the time he was shooting RIVALS OF KUNG FU, someone at the studio told him he looked and moved like the late Bruce Lee. Huang replied back, "I look and move like Huang Chien Lung!" This exchange must've recurred to Huang a few years later, giving him the idea to re-brand himself as a Bruce Lee imitator since it was working fairly well internationally for Ho Chung Tao, alias Bruce Li.

Since most of Huang's movies where he's billed as Bruce Le never played theaters in Hong Kong, it's difficult to find information on them as periodicals of the day seldom mentioned him; nor was he listed among some 160 leading actors working in Hong Kong in 1978. The rarest of his HK productions was, ironically, among the most publicized back in the day; and seemingly, Bruce Le wasn't initially among the cast.

THE BIG BOSS 2 (THE SECOND BROTHER FROM TANGSHAN in Chinese) began filming in 1976; it was funded by entrepreneur Chow Yi Fung (Zhou Yi Feng) and his HK Skylight Film Company (Tian Xiang Films). Mr. Chow was apparently far more successful in the aviation and shipping industries than his foray into the film world. His production house only made three movies before it shut down--the biggest of these being CHINA ARMED ESCORT aka THE BODYGUARD starring Taiwanese TV and movie actress, producer, writer and director, Pearl Cheung Ling. She was a martial artist who found international fame in a trilogy of Wuxia fantasies--WOLF DEVIL WOMAN (WOLFEN NINJA), MATCHING ESCORT (VENUS THE NINJA) and MIRACULOUS FLOWER (PHOENIX THE NINJA).

Strangely, THE BIG BOSS 2 was among the most heavily promoted Bruceploitation pictures at the time and has since become the hardest of the sub-genre to find. Judging by multiple articles about its filming in 1976, Bruce Le wasn't listed as part of the original cast. It's possible his scenes were added and shot some time later. Director Chan Chue had a legitimate Lee association; he'd been both an actor and the AD on the original

THE BIG BOSS in 1971.

Exterior filming took place in Thailand. Actress Wang Ping (KING BOXER; THE SISTER OF THE SHANTUNG BOXER) was hired as the female lead due to her popularity there. In the end, THE BIG BOSS 2 allegedly cost over HK$1 million to make and only brought in HK$82,661 in 6 days when it was released in Hong Kong in 1978.

Apparently, Lo Lieh and Bruce Le would shoot the fan favorite BRUCE'S DEADLY FINGERS (1976) around the same time. This one makes about as much sense as most Bruce Le flicks. Large chunks of this movie would turn up in BRUCE'S NINJA SECRET, aka BRUCE'S LAST BATTLE; a movie strung together using equally large amounts of footage from Joseph Kong's Filipino lensed BRUCE AND THE SHAOLIN BRONZEMEN (1982); one of the wackiest of the Bruce Clone pictures.

Many of Bruce Le's movies didn't play in Hong Kong. He frequently worked in every other Asian market making approximately two dozen movies for P.T. Insantra Films--owned by Robert Jeffrey (Robert Theh) and Duncan Leong. This cooperation would give Huang Chien Lung a major boost on the international market by the start of the 1980s.

By the mid-70s in Southeast Asia, cooperation between territories was not only beneficial but necessary.

In 1976, Hong Kong and Indonesia formed partnerships with their respective countries for filmmaking endeavors after film industries in Southeast Asia were hit hard by the oil crisis, the television market, and Vietnam falling to the communists--resulting in the loss of that market and others like the Khmer Republic. Moreover, the Philippines then unified with China so that affected the industry as well. The 22nd Asian Film Festival, for example, was supposed to have been held there but it was reassigned to be held in South Korea due to the political conflict.

As a result, other Asian territories decided to focus their resources on building their domestic product and imposed regulations on film imports from Hong Kong. This in turn affected the selling of HK movies to other countries like Thailand and Indonesia. So now, distributors became more selective on what titles they chose to pay licenses for. They also became more stringent on the types of movies they purchased. With the growing emphasis on stronger scenes of sex and violence, such films were frowned upon outside Hong Kong. Naturally, there would be multiple versions made exclusively for the various censor-prone markets that now had tighter restrictions than before.

On March 15th, 1976, a delegation of five film stars and four representatives from Cinemart Magazine were invited for the opening ceremony of the first color film laboratory in Indonesia, called P.T. International Cine and Studio Center, Limited. This was to be a bridge between the two territories for mutual cooperation in their industries. Among the stars present for the ceremony were Chen Kuan Tai, James Yi Lei, Li Ching, and Shaw Yin Yin.

Bruce Le would greatly benefit from this by making many incredibly cheap action pictures not just in Indonesia, but South Korea, Thailand and the Philippines. His movies were largely ignored in Hong Kong, and the few that weren't made little money there.

By 1977, Bruce Le had entered the Dragon sweepstakes and made what seemed like a million movies aping everything memorable

about Bruce Lee's films. The actor made over a dozen pictures utilizing various iconography from Lee's limited filmography. Le's catalog is also confusing in the most frustrating way with a myriad of interchangeable titles, multiple versions, and mix n' match edits. His films never had much in the way of narratives either. What passed for plots in Le's movies was bare minimum and built around an endless stream of fight sequences.

To add even more confusion, foreign distributors would market these films to give the impression Bruce Le was starring in a picture he wasn't actually in. One example is the German promotion for 1978s STORMING ATTACKS starring Bruce Li and John Cheung. Marketed as BRUCE LEE THE RAVENOUS COUGAR (see top image), the distributors decided to deceive patrons into thinking Bruce Le was also starring in the movie by putting his face on the advertising. Another example is a version of the French publicity for BRUCE LI IN NEW GUINEA (1979) as BRUCE LEE IN NEW GUINEA (see insert). It's a Bruce Li picture but this particular bit of promotion gives the impression both Li and Le are starring together!

One of Huang Chien Lung's films that played HK theaters was BRUCE AND SHAOLIN KUNG FU (1977). A P.T. Insantra production funded with Indonesian and South Korean financing, it featured many familiar faces both in front of, and behind, the camera. Actors James Nam (who also co-directs), Chiang Tao and Bolo Yeung appear while Joseph Kong acts as a screenwriter. Shaolin movies were big business between 1976-1978 so Bruce and his financiers were keen to chop off a share of the monastery market for themselves.

When BRUCE AND SHAOLIN KUNG FU was released in HK in 1978, it only made HK$90,615. Astonishingly, it was kept in theaters for 7 days. This longer run for a pittance box office take may be due to the film only playing English theater lines. HK theaters that played movies made by or for foreigners tended to stay in theaters longer than local product.

Despite not making money in HK, it must've made money elsewhere because a sequel was released the same year; likely shot simultaneously. The first film managed to get a Japanese release at the tail end of the Karate Boom there, released as FIST OF FURY PART 2. To accentuate how these imitator films were largely made for foreign audiences, the word 'Bruce' is nowhere to be found in the Chinese titles. Part one is called BODHIDHARMA IRON FINGER KUNG FU while part 2 is titled BURNING AT THE GATES OF SHAOLIN.

When GAME OF DEATH (1978) was finally completed and released in 1978 by Golden Harvest, it was arguably the most polished Bruceploitation motion picture yet made. Unintentionally funny and as offensive as any of the no-budget imitator flicks, this was the second of three times Raymond Chow produced a movie banking money from the dead superstar. The first was the 1973 Lee documentary that Chow rushed into theaters, BRUCE LEE, THE MAN AND THE LEGEND; then GAME OF DEATH; and then GAME OF DEATH 2, aka TOWER OF DEATH (1981).

GAME OF DEATH 2 was reported to have begun filming in the summer of 1978 with shooting having commenced in Japan and Yasuaki Kurata starring. It was also reported that director Ng See Yuen was using outtakes from Bruce's movies to formulate whatever the plot of the film was originally supposed to be. Director Ng remained attached to the project but Kurata didn't by the time the film started up again in 1980.

TOWER OF DEATH (1981) is certainly exploitative but easily a better movie than its even more embarrassing predecessor. Korean martial artist Kim Tai Chung, aka Tong Long (not to be confused with Lou Rei's older brother), was Lee's stand-in on GAME OF DEATH (1978) and played his ghost in NO RETREAT, NO SURRENDER (1986). Like many others, there was nothing about Kim that resembled the dead Kung Fu star. As it were, Hong Kong audiences showed an equal amount of disinterest in TOWER OF DEATH as they did most of the others in the late 1970s.

Bruce Le, who was always game for riding a bandwagon, would do his own version of GAME OF DEATH in what would be one of his more popular movies.

ENTER THE GAME OF DEATH is not good but it's endlessly entertaining; especially the action sequences inside the "pagoda", that is nothing more than a small office lit with different color lighting each time Bruce takes on a new opponent. Like most Le movies, there's barely a plot and what little is there is held flimsily together by near constant fight scenes. A co-production with South Korea, it apparently got a HK release in 1981 after Le had attracted attention in America in 1980 when his films were being shown on television, ENTER being the first.

By the start of the new decade in 1980, mainstream theater play for Kung Fu films had vanished. Drive-in's and their seedier major city equivalents were safe havens; but Chinese Fist n' Kickers would have to find a new, more stable home.

The owners of P.T. Insantra then struck a deal with Roy Winnick, proprietor of Best Film and Video Corporation, to release Bruce's Insantra catalog in America. If you grew up in the 1980s, you surely saw a multitude of Bruce Le pictures in K-mart in the VHS section; and in video stores across the country. Winnick then licensed the titles for television syndication. This, of course, was

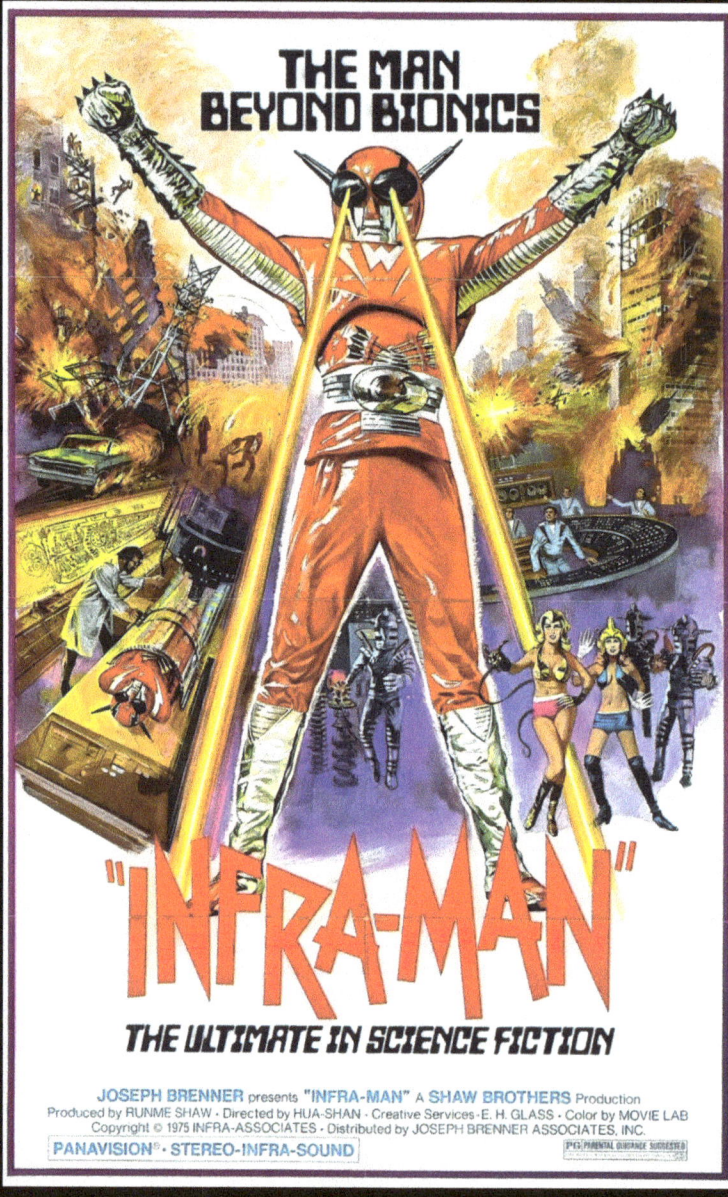

around the same time the Black Belt Theater packages hit the airwaves in what became the second Kung Fu Boom in America.

Another of Bruce's films that played HK was his most ambitious feature at the time, 1981s BRUCE STRIKES BACK; ambitious in scope and not its funding. It was promoted as being the first Kung Fu picture fully funded by European producers but directed by a Chinese; that being Bruce Le and apparently an un-credited Joseph Kong, a frequent collaborator with Bruce who also went by the name of Joseph Velasco.

One of the highlights of the movie was the final fight with Korean kicking sensation Hwang Jang Lee taking place inside the Roman Colosseum; something that hadn't been allowed before. Bruce Lee got some shots of the famed locale for his final duel in WAY OF THE DRAGON (1972), but the actual fight was shot inside a studio. The budget for Le's globe-trotting KF adventure was only US$50,000.

Actor and bodybuilder Yang Tze, aka Bolo Yeung, was a frequent performer in Bruce Le's movies. Bolo had taken a role as a bodyguard in ENTER THE DRAGON (1973) after he and Bruce Lee met on the set of a cigarette commercial for Winston cigarettes. Lee was promoting his movie WAY OF THE DRAGON and he and the strongman became friends. Unfortunately, we never got to see the two men fight in the released version of ENTER THE DRAGON, but Bolo was nevertheless an integral part of the mythos; so fans got to see the muscleman battle the fake one many times. You never saw him in Bruce Li's films so Bruce Le rectified this by fitting him in whenever possible.

To the detriment of already shoddy productions, Bolo was rarely ever utilized sufficiently in those films; he would get a fight scene or two and be defeated far too quickly. There may have been reasons for this; like his out of the blue appearance in fan favorite BRUCE'S DEADLY FINGERS (1976). Bolo's screen-time amounts to about five minutes, which may have been simply a favor while he was on a break from filming another movie a few blocks down.

Whether for good or ill, the mass exportation of cheap Kung Fu pictures killed off the genres theatrical staying power in overseas markets. The most likely scenario is that audience tastes and expectations for how movies were made changed due to STAR WARS in 1977. Mainstream viewers had moved on while the Drive-in and 42nd Street crowds remained. In 1978, even HK journalists were noting that if Chinese filmmakers wanted to maintain and even increase the US market for their KF films, they needed to make fewer of them and increase the quality or else they will lose what little market share they had at the time.

Like the moniker "Spaghetti Western", a label that later became a term of endearment, the Kung Fu flick had a far more condescending and derogatory term applied, that being "Chopsocky". Further, the plethora of dubbed KF flicks snatched up on an almost daily basis did nothing to change casual viewers and critics perceptions of these movies. Leading the charge was the seemingly endless series of pictures starring Bruce Le.

The enterprising Lee-alike had successfully made the move to the US home video and burgeoning cable television market. TV became the new home of Kung Fu via Black Belt Theater packages. Made up mostly of Shaw Brothers pictures, there was an occasional Bruce-ish flick mixed in like DYNAMO (1978) and barely bio's like BRUCE LEE'S WAYS OF KUNG FU. Video store shelves were stocked full of titles from companies like Saturn Video, Master Arts, All Seasons Entertainment and Unicorn Video to name a few. Among them were a proliferation of Bruce Le flicks like BRUCE LE'S GREATEST REVENGE, BRUCE VS. BILL, BRUCE THE SUPERHERO, and BRUCE'S FISTS OF VENGEANCE to name a few. Bruce Le was also a director, and guided himself in a handful of his

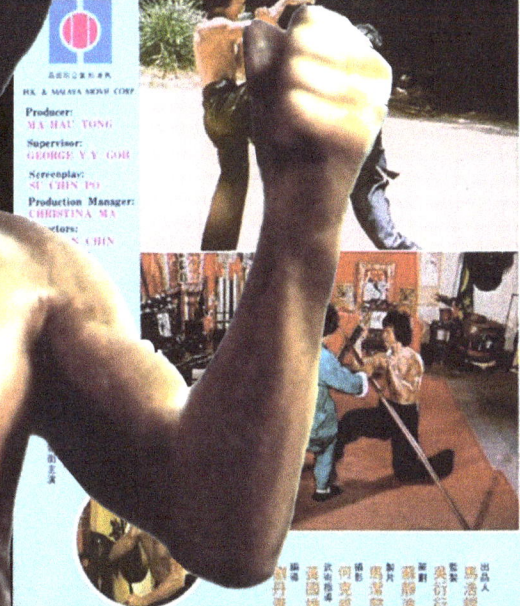

Pretend Lee pictures. He famously turned up in the Euro-US gore-horror spectacle, PIECES (1983). Produced by Dick Randall, Bruce was a close friend of the American exploitation peddler, so he got a bizarre cameo appearing on-camera with Lynda Day George. Le's career includes movies that are outside the Bruce Lee Imitator spectrum like THE MAD COLD-BLOODED MURDER (1981) and THE SUPER GANG (1982), but it's the incredibly cheap, barely decipherable Bruce-a-thon's that fans remember best.

There were many more Heirs of the Dragon and others important to his legacy...

ATTACK OF THE CLONES: A COLLECTION OF OTHER BRUCE LEE'S & CONNECTIONS

1. From Korea came Dragon Lee, aka Moon Kyoung Seok (or Keo Ryong); one of the top three most recognizable and prolific of the actual Bruce Lee clone actors. The Korean Dragon is very popular among Kung Fu fans although few of his movies played in HK theaters; those being films like *KUNG FU FEVER* (1979) and fan favorite, *THE CLONES OF BRUCE LEE* (1980). *DRAGON ON FIRE* (1979), alias *THE DRAGON, THE HERO* is another. It's not a leading part for Dragon Lee, but was promoted as one in some areas.

Directed by Godfrey Ho, it's memorable for the infamous scene where a dog bites off Chan Lau's penis. It's actually John Liu (Liu Chung Chiang) in the leading role. Liu was from Taiwan and studied Japanese arts winning tournaments at 14 years old. He's also reported to have defeated Chuck Norris in Paris during a live event in 1976. Liu was discovered by Ng See Yuen through European martial arts magazines. He called Paris home and taught his own style there, Zen Kwan Do. John Liu is popular among fans, but he was never a major star in Hong Kong. In some markets, it appears John Liu was billed as Bruce Lei. *THE DRAGON, THE HERO* is the only movie John Liu did with a Bruce impersonator.

Some of the bulkier Dragon's most enjoyable entries had him co-starring with Korean super-kicking sensation Hwang Jang Lee; three of their South Korean-made movies being *SECRET NINJA, ROARING TIGER* (1982), *MARTIAL MONKS OF SHAOLIN TEMPLE* and *5-PATTERN DRAGON CLAWS* (both 1983). These productions showcase lots of HJL kicking action and Dragon Lee in fine form.

Built like a brick wall, Dragon Lee was a more lithe version of Bolo Yeung. He looked like he regularly lifted weights while Bolo had a body akin to a power-lifter. Whenever Dragon Lee did his Bruce impersonations it looked comical, particularly when he'd shake his head wildly. Even when he was doing films not marketed as a Bruce clone work, some of Lee's mannerisms crept in anyway.

Easily the most popular movie to star Dragon Lee was *THE CLONES OF BRUCE LEE* (1980). It also starred Bruce Le and Bruce Lai, alias Kwok Si Chi. The latter Lee-alike had been a bit player in some Shaw Brothers pictures and *CLONES* was his biggest role. Of the three Lee's featured, he looks the least like the Little Dragon. *CLONES* is a favorite of many for its kooky story, non-stop action, send-up of spy movies and the HK film industry itself.

2. Taiwanese actor Lung Tien Sheng mimicked Lee in some of his early movies like *THE REVENGE DRAGON* (1973). By the end of the decade he was doing it again in 1979s *SEA GIRLS* or, as it was also known in Asian territories *BRUCE LEE AGAINST SNAKE IN THE EAGLE'S SHADOW*; that title cashing in on both the Lee name as well as the explosion of Jackie Chan--who in 1978 had found the fame he'd been looking for in Yuen Woo Ping's *SNAKE IN THE EAGLE'S SHADOW*; and to a greater degree, in *DRUNKEN MASTER* (both 1978).

That same year in 1979, Lung Tien Sheng would play Bruce Lee in *THE TRUE GAME*

OF DEATH; and did a surprisingly good job in the role. On a par with the utter ridiculousness of this sub-genre, some Chinese posters pasted Lung's head onto Lee's body in an image taken from ENTER THE DRAGON; while other versions of the poster used the unobstructed image of Bruce Lee in the same pose. This example of false advertising may have been inspired by the infamous shot in GAME OF DEATH where an image of Bruce Lee's head is taped to a mirror concealing the actor's real face.

By the end of December in '79, Lung Tien Sheng would be at Shaw Brothers Studio in Hong Kong to start re-shoots on Chang Cheh's TEN TIGERS OF KWANGTUNG (1980) and play a leading role in Chang's FLAG OF IRON (1980). He was a known actor in Taiwan, but in Hong Kong, he was a new face. Possessing a lot of charisma, he unfortunately never hit the big time in Hong Kong. His portrayal of Bruce Lee remains an underrated performance.

3 FIST OF FEAR, TOUCH OF DEATH (1980) stands out from virtually every other movie in the Bruce impersonator sub-genre; and that's not because it's a good movie. Depending on one's point of view, Matthew Mallinson's 1980 flick is either one of the most entertaining or the most tasteless of the lot. It also stands out by not having an actual clone in the movie, but Lee himself!

What's wildly offensive about it (or hilarious, again depending on your POV) is that it utilizes old footage of Lee as a young teenager and adult and dubs new, totally unrelated dialog over the footage. There's also footage of the Taiwan-lensed Swordplay feature FORCED TO FIGHT, released here as THE INVINCIBLE SUPER CHAN, that is used to tell the story of how Bruce's grandfather was a samurai warrior! It showed that American producers could milk the Lee name as deceptively as the Chinese producers; it's a one-of-a-kind movie that must be seen to be believed. The reason for the sub-genres existence was to mine as much money off the dead superstar as possible. Before his death, the hope was to find an actor that could compete with Lee. After, it was finding one who could mimic him.... it wasn't just the men, either.

4 In February of 1973, journalists were referring to actress Chia Ling (Judy Lee) as "the female Bruce Lee". She was a hot commodity in Taiwan after an impressive debut in QUEEN BOXER (1972) aka THE AVENGER (HATRED in Chinese). In this picture, Chia Ling plays Ma Su Chen, the sister to Ma Yung Chen of the HK box office sensation BOXER FROM SHANTUNG starring Chen Kuan Tai and directed by the venerable Chang Cheh. A discovery of actor-filmmaker Peter Yang Chun, Chia Ling was a student of the Fu Shing Drama School. She studied Peking Opera alongside classmates Angela Mao Ying and Charlie Chin Hsiang Lin for a ten year period.

Signing with HK Fong Ming Motion Pictures in 1971, it was a new independent company founded by the husband and wife team of Yang Chun and Florence Yu. They had Chia Ling doing martial arts demonstrations on television before introducing her to movie audiences in THE AVENGER and THE ESCAPE, both directed by Florence Yu and released in 1972. THE AVENGER (released in America as QUEEN BOXER where she was promoted as "the female Bruce Lee" on the poster) purportedly made more money in Taiwan, but was the most profitable of the BOXER FROM SHANTUNG spin-offs in Hong Kong. It held out for 11 days in theaters, bringing in HK$753,121 at the end of its run there. In 1973, Chia Ling told journalist Annie Wong, "My greatest wish in this industry is to be a good actor, and not a movie star". Chia Ling stayed busy in movies the entirety of the 1970s.

5 When Bruce Lee died, there were already numerous other big stars and many hit films; the desire was for a new performer that could hit the off-the-chart box office highs for action movies in the HK$3-HK$5 million range the way Lee did. That didn't come till 1978 and from Jackie Chan, a one-time pseudo Bruce imitator and an actor whose action movie style was the exact opposite of Bruce Lee. Lo Wei tried turning Chan into an assortment of genre personas from heroes to a villain. His first flick for Lo Wei was an attempt to recapture an earlier glory with *NEW FIST OF FURY* (1976), which was discussed earlier.

Chan's success at the end of the decade eventually led to the destruction of the traditional Kung Fu movie. Like Lee, Chan was even more obsessed with topping himself; and in so doing, he killed the genre off, then brought it back again in a different form in the early 80s with films like DRAGON LORD (1982) and PROJECT A (1983). In reference to both men, Bruce Le's company, Dragon Films, distributed a Bruce-Jackie combo clone flick called BRUCE AND JACKIE TO THE RESCUE (1981).

6 Another HK Kung Fu flick that was re-packaged in America as a Bruce Lee styled motion picture was 1972s KUNG FU, THE INVISIBLE FIST aka THE GOOD AND THE BAD starring Chen Sing and Yasuaki Kurata. The latter was a Japanese Karate master whom Chang Cheh gave a career in Hong Kong KF movies to after putting him in THE ANGRY GUEST that same year. The poster for KUNG FU, THE INVISIBLE FIST had the most instructive tagline of all the US Kung Fu releases that repeatedly confused the Chinese and Japanese arts with, "Learn the difference between Karate and Kung Fu!"

Later re-titled THE REAL DRAGON, Kurata was then marketed as Sonny Bruce--equal parts Sonny Chiba and Bruce Lee. Kurata was also being promoted as Bruce Lo for THE DRAGONS CLAW, a Japanese Karate picture titled WHICH IS STRONGER, KARATE OR TIGER? (1976). Kurata has the distinction of being the sole Japanese film actor in the American distribution of Chinese-language movies to have two monikers milking the Bruce Lee lineage.

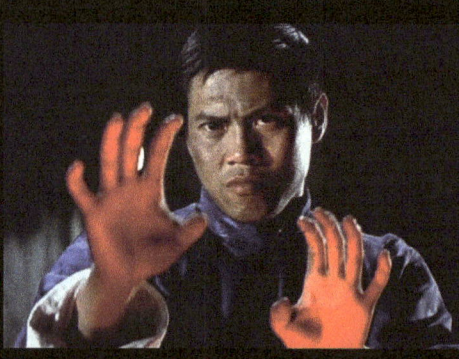

7 It was *KING BOXER* (1972) that started the world's fascination with Kung Fu movies in 1973. But in Japan, what really caused the Karate Boom in Nipponese society was Bruce Lee. Several dozen Chinese martial arts flicks were scooped up and released in Japan in 1974 after ENTER THE DRAGON was a smash hit there. This inspired Toei executives and superstar Sonny Chiba to produce their own martial arts actioners. The boom lasted from 1974-1977; and by 1978, period-set Samurai sagas took control. Bruce Lee, though, was still very popular in Japan with re-releases of his films bringing in good box office. In the Land of the Rising Sun, the Clones were no substitute for the real thing. Among the last of the Karate pictures was *VIOLENT DEATH! WAY OF THE EVIL FIST* (1977), known elsewhere as SOUL OF CHIBA

and SOUL OF BRUCE LEE. Independently co-financed by stars Sonny Chiba and Tadashi Yamashita, this Thai-shot actioner co-stars Bolo Yeung, Etsuko Shihomi and Shikamura Ito, aka Lu Chuan; a Japanese martial artist who worked frequently in Hong Kong, and primarily at Shaw Studio.

Outside Japan, Tadashi Yamashita had a brief flirtation with the Bruce Clone movement. In America, New Line Cinema had some degree of success with the first in his trilogy known in Japan as THE KARATE (1974-1975). It was re-titled for US release as BRONSON LEE, CHAMPION. The film must've been popular elsewhere because Tadashi co-starred alongside Yasuaki Kurata in a Hong Kong movie produced by indy company Goldig titled THE MAGNIFICENT 3 (1980). For the HK promotion, and other territories, Tadashi was billed as Bronson Lee. Just as Bruce Lee had been, Charles Bronson was very popular in Hong Kong.

8 Henry Yu Yang, star of 1973s *THE AWAKEN PUNCH* (or *EARTH-SHATTERING FIST*), became an unwitting Bruce Lee knock-off in America. The 1974 film *THE BRAVE LION* was re-titled *REVOLT OF THE DRAGON* for stateside release. The film's poster infers the movie is about the late Bruce Lee, using an image of Henry Yu Yang who isn't even in the movie. The still used for the poster is from the 1974 Kung Fu Comedy *WITS TO WITS*. Continuing Henry Yu's tenuous Lee connection, he co-starred with Chen Sing in 1972s *TOUGH GUY*. In America, *TOUGH GUY* was re-titled *KUNG FU MASTER: BRUCE LEE STYLE*; the poster featuring an image of the Little Dragon in the top corner.

A graduate of Shaw Brothers Nanguo Experimental Theater Troupe, he declined signing with the company and went with Cathay Pictures, the other major company in HK at that time. When they shut down in 1971, Yu Yang went the indy route. A student

Bruce Lee Special Vol.2 No.5 29

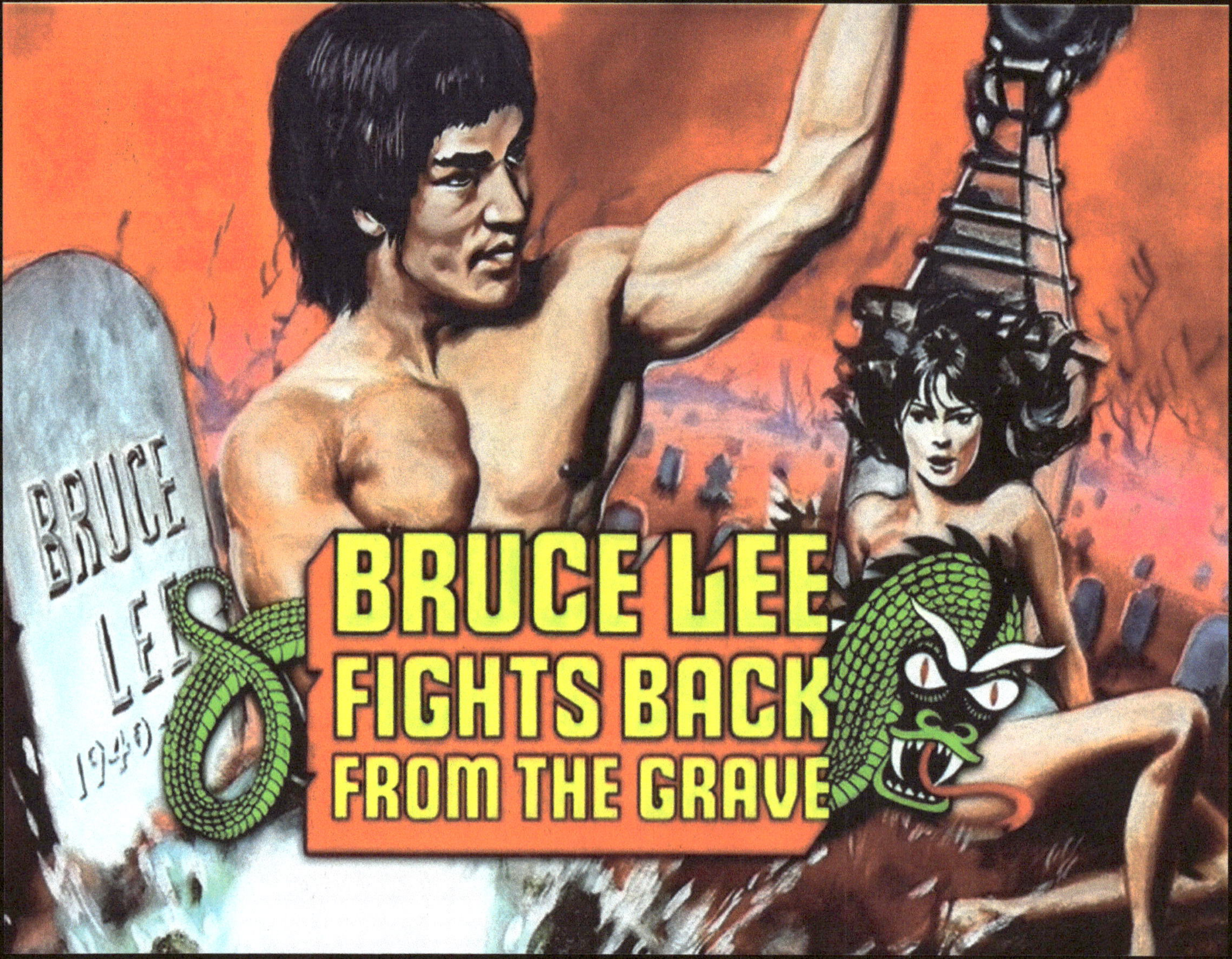

BRUCE LEE FIGHTS BACK FROM THE GRAVE

of his AWAKEN PUNCH co-star Fang Yeh, he co-starred in Ng See Yuen's surprise hit THE BLOODY FISTS in 1972 alongside former Shaw support player and new leading man Chen Sing. Henry Yu Yang, though, wasn't an imposing figure on-camera; so the actor whose leading man status took off was his co-star Chen Sing. It's important to note that Yu Yang wasn't being promoted as a new Bruce Lee in Hong Kong; he was only being pushed as a new action star there.

9 One actor who was being quietly pushed as "Bruce Lee number 2" at Golden Harvest was Korean martial artist Byong Yu. He looked nothing like Lee in any way, but apparently the producers saw something in him that resonated the late JKD founder. The company's own publication, Golden Movie News, heavily promoted Byong's expertise in the arts in the hopes he would stand out in an already crowded field. After a star turn in the modern day thriller called THE ASSOCIATION (1975), it was one-and-done for Byong Yu's movie career.

10 Then there was the 1976 Korean Kung Fu fight-fest VISITOR TO AMERICA starring Korean TKD expert Jun Chong. That title doesn't exactly scream action so Aquarius Releasing gave it a new name and a wacky opening scene to match the thoroughly bizarre title they saddled it with--BRUCE LEE FIGHTS BACK FROM THE GRAVE. It's worth a watch to see an early performance by future ninja sensation Sho Kosugi (see insert with Jun Chong).

When he was a boy, Jun Chong's mother encouraged him to learn martial arts although he had little interest in it. This was amplified when he suffered a broken arm during his training. He persevered and eventually won a gold medal in Korea's Olympic games in 1964. He came to America in 1966 and by 1970, Jun Chong was teaching TKD. Unlike Bruce Lee, Jun competed in tournaments and won the USA National TKD Tournament's Grand Championship in 1972.

When Jun first became interested in making movies, he auditioned for the role of Bruce Lee in Robert Clouse's abandoned Bruce bi-

opic 'Tribute To Bruce Lee', later called 'The Life and Legend of Bruce Lee'. According to Jun in a 1976 interview, after VISITOR TO

brother to Alexander Lo (or Lou or Luo) of movies like *INCREDIBLE KUNG FU MISSION* (1980), *NEW SOUTHERN FISTS NORTHERN KICKS* (1981), *SHAOLIN VS. NINJA* (1983), *SHAOLIN VS. LAMA* (1983) and *MAFIA VS. NINJA* (1985). Since very little is known about him, this section can expand on who he was and his Chinese Connection to the Lee-alike sub-genre.

Lo the elder came from a martial arts family and studied TKD in Taiwan. He had a two year period as a leading man before dropping out of the industry and reappearing in 1976. In 1974, Tong Lung became friends with former-actor-turned-filmmaker Lan Tien Hong. Mr. Lan would produce Tong's last movie during his leading man phase with *THE BEST OF THE WORST* (1974), aka *CAPTURE THE KILLER* for his Lan Tien Motion Picture Company. Lan's connection to Tong also extends to the Bruce clone movement as he was the producer of *THE STORY OF THE DRAGON* (1976), aka *BRUCE LEE'S SECRET*, aks *BRUCE LEE'S DEADLY KUNG FU*--starring Ho Chung Tao and Carter Wong. It was through producer Lan that Tong's brother (also a MA champion), Lou Rei, got into the film industry where he would then meet Robert Tai Chi Hsien.

The younger Luo brother debuted in Robert Tai's *DEVIL KILLER* (1981), a film that was largely made up of scenes from his older brother's *CAPTURE THE KILLER* from 1974. All four men--Lan Tien Hong, Tong Lung, Lou Rei, and Robert Tai--worked on this picture together and on subsequent films after it. Tong never had a major leading role upon his return to the industry, but he did

AMERICA was a big hit in his native Korea, he returned home and made two additional films, 'The Kingdom' and 'Triple Agency', but never learned if either picture played theaters in his homeland or anywhere else. By 1980, Jun Chong had went back to teaching his growing number of students (in the thousands) and never acted again.

11 Then there was a Hawaiian martial artist named Myron Lee who co-starred with *ENTER THE DRAGON*'s Jim Kelly in *DEATH DIMENSION* (1978) directed by Al Adamson. The cast featured two James Bond alums including one-time 007 George Lazenby; Harold Sakata was the other. As for Myron, he was re-named Myron BRUCE Lee for the film's advertising. Like other potential heirs to the KF crown, Myron never did another movie.

12 In Part One, the first so-called Bruce Lee imitator came from Taiwan; that man being Luo Zhen, or Lo Chen (not to be confused with Lo Chen the film director), or Tong Lung, better known as the older

receive leading villain roles in a handful of Robert Tai's movies like SHAOLIN CHASTITY KUNG FU (1983) and MAFIA VS NINJA (1985). He should be remembered as one of, if not the first actor, to be marketed as a Bruce Lee-style action star in both Chinese-speaking territories and overseas markets.

13 In 1975, it was announced that Robert Clouse would direct a Warner Brothers documentary about Bruce Lee's life titled 'Tribute To Bruce Lee'. It was to have been based on Linda Lee's 1975 book, 'Bruce Lee: The Man Only I Knew'. The actor chosen to play Lee was a 23 year old martial artist named Alex Kwon. Born in Hong Kong as Kwok Ki Chung, he had studied the Northern KF style, My Jhong Law Horn, since he was 6 years old. What was immediately evident, and something that wasn't lost on Warner executives, was that Kwon didn't look like Bruce Lee; nor was his traditional Kung Fu style remotely similar to Lee's JKD, a style that abandoned traditional Chinese fighting forms.

Ultimately, this film was never made. Allegedly, neither Linda Lee nor director Clouse could agree on details of the production so they parted ways. The ENTER THE DRAGON director would return to Hong Kong to begin work finishing Lee's THE GAME OF DEATH (1978) at Golden Harvest in 1977. In 1993, Linda Lee Cadwell's book 'Bruce Lee: The Man Only I Knew' would finally be brought to the screen as DRAGON: THE BRUCE LEE STORY with Jason Scott Lee (no relation) in the role of the Dragon. Linda Lee would write another book about her late husband in 1989 titled 'The Bruce Lee Story'. As for Alex Kwon, he reportedly moved to London where he went back to training students in the martial arts.

14 Bruce's wife, Linda Lee Cadwell, is also an important, if unwitting, individual in this much-maligned sub-genre. You would occasionally see some occidental actress playing her in some of these films. Linda Lee sued the American producers/distributors of some of the Bruce clone movies for using her late husband's likeness without the estate's permission. Two films were cited-- 1974s SUPER DRAGON, aka THE DRAGON DIES HARD and 1976s CHINESE CHIEH CHUAN KUNG FU, aka BRUCE LEE: SUPER DRAGON. The Los Angeles Superior Court ordered Allied Artists, Hallmark Productions, Esquire Productions and Winthrop Amusements to pay $25,000 to Lee's estate. When it came to the exploitation of her husband in Hong Kong, Linda Lee was reported to have objected to, then quietly dropped her rejection towards, the release of BRUCE LEE, THE MAN AND THE LEGEND (1973); the documentary Raymond Chow rushed into theaters a few months after Lee's passing.

Curiously, Linda was friendly with Bruce's paramour, Betty Ting Pei. At a court hearing about Bruce's death in October of 1973, Linda was seen holding Betty's hand. The following day she attracted more attention by personally taking Ting Pei to dinner. With Betty next to her, she made a public statement for citizens to please not believe the stories of Bruce and Betty, citing their friendship for the past year. This was a futile attempt to calm the fury of the public that felt a seething hatred towards Ting Pei. In 1981, Betty Ting Pei revealed in an interview that she and Linda remained friends and that she had written her a letter after Bruce's death and that she would never reveal its contents.

15 Then there's Robert Lee (Li Zhen Hui, or Li Jun Fai), Bruce's younger brother. He chose a different career path from his older, more famous brother. A popular HK musician in the mid to late 1960s, he would move to the United States in 1969 to go to college. While there, he took computer courses. In 1975, he recorded an album dedicated to his late sibling titled 'The Ballad of Bruce Lee'. Robert Lee would return to Hong Kong in 1976 for singing engagements and to sign a three-picture deal with Golden Harvest. The reason he signed with the company was he wanted to make a film about his relationship with Bruce Lee. Raymond Chow had other plans, putting the singer and would-be actor in two comedies co-starring with Sylvia Chang. It was reported in 1978 that Robert was soon to begin shooting 'The Dragon's Brother' for the company. Announced as being directed by LADY WHIRLWIND's Huang Feng (sometimes listed as Wong Fung, but not the same Wong Fung that discovered Bruce Le), filming was to have taken place in Holland, South Korea and Macau. The younger Lee did do one more movie for the Central Motion Picture Company, A TITLE RE-WON (1979), a film that looks like a Chinese version of ROCKY (1976). Robert Lee did finally do a film about his brother's life in the 2010 Hong Kong film, BRUCE LEE, MY BROTHER.

16 One martial artist who is often referred to as a Lee impersonator

wasn't technically one of them; but did play Bruce Lee in one of the more rare and popular clone pictures. Bruce Liang was the real deal. The son of a well known martial arts instructor, Liang Hsiao Leung (Liang Hsiao Lung) starred in THE DRAGON LIVES AGAIN (1977), his one time playing Lee in what amounted to a playful spoof that was intended to be a tribute of sorts to the late superstar. The rumor that his penis was hard at death is visualized for tastelessly comedic effect here. There's no plot to speak of other than Lee goes to Hell and meets a variety of famous film and pop culture characters like Zatoichi, Popeye, The Exorcist, Emmanuelle, The Man With No Name, the One Armed Swordsman, etc, and fights mummies and skeletons. Like most of these impersonator flicks, moviegoers in Hong Kong weren't all that interested in the Dragon's resurrection as depicted in Law Chi's cult favorite. It made HK$423,932 in six days.

17 Director To Lo Po has the distinction of shooting movies starring the Big Three--Bruce Li, Bruce Le and Dragon Lee. He started his career helming RETURN OF THE HERO OF THE WATERFRONT (1973), and would later direct BRUCE AND THE IRON FINGER (1979), a movie with ambiguous connections to the Little Dragon. The Chinese title (BIG MASTER AND THE PROSTITUTE) zeroes in on the film's Kung Fu Murder Mystery plot, while the English export title gives the impression you're in for some Lee-alike action. Billed under his real name in the Chinese release, Ho Chung Tao plays a cop named Bruce. Co-starring with him is Bruce Liang (Liang Hsiao Lung). It's an unusual actioner that's worth your time if you're a KF fan.

Director To also directed JEET KUNE THE CLAWS AND THE SUPREME KUNG FU (1979), aka FIST OF FURY III, discussed in PART 1; and BRUCE LE'S GREATEST REVENGE (1979), another FIST OF FURY styled do-over. To Lo Po then guided Dragon Lee in two Clone pictures, DRAGON BRUCE LEE PART 2 and DRAGON LEE FIGHTS AGAIN (both 1981). The former is another FIST OF FURY type actioner even though it also goes by the title of BIG BOSS 2, confusingly enough. You'll see Bolo battling the Dragon in this one. The latter title is also known as MUSCLE OF THE DRAGON. Shot entirely in Korea, it's a Filmline Production that has footage from THE CLONES OF BRUCE LEE (also a Filmline picture) inserted into it. Some of the film's advertising

uses images of Bruce Le from CLONES.

Another vital figure in the American Kung Fu craze and Bruce Lee Mania phase in the 1970s was producer-distributor Serafim Karalexis. Closing out this two-part article series are 10 questions on his career in the business of releasing Kung Fu films in America.

10 QUESTIONS WITH SERAFIM KERALEXIS

VENOMS5: How did your interest in importing and producing Kung Fu movies start?

SERAFIM KARALEXIS: I saw *5 FINGERS OF DEATH* and the next morning I was on a flight to Hong Kong to acquire a martial arts film for distribution. I distributed the second martial arts film in the US, a Shaw Brothers film, *THE DUEL*, that I retitled *DUEL OF THE IRON FIST*.

V5: What sort of man was Yang Man Yi? For an indy company he had a steady number of films coming out per year. What was the average budget of a Yang Tze picture?

SK: I knew him as Yeo Ban Yee, though his name was pronounced differently by different people. He was a very nice person, polite, courteous and a man of his word. We made deals on a handshake. He owned a film developing laboratory and he produced a number of low-budget films, lower than Shaw Brothers, though I don't know the exact amount of his average budget, since they varied.

V5: He made several movies in South Korea with Jason Pai Piao and Tony (Tommy) Lu. Did you get to know them well?

SK: Yeo Ban Yee made films all over Asia, including South Korea, Malaysia, the Philippines, and HK, and possibly other places. His interest was to show a variety of locations and of course to find the best production value to produce the film. Jason Pai Piao, Tommy Loo Chung and other actors were used by Yeo for a number of films. I got to know them well, since I was on the set everyday and we would go out to dinner. Thompson Kao Kang also came to New York where I used him in *DEATH PROMISE* with Charles Bonet.

V5: Did you interact much with cast and crew--and if so, were there any difficulties due to cultural differences?

SK: I was there on a daily basis, while the film was being produced. Most of the guys were somewhat westernized, due to HK being a British colony and they spoke English well. Tommy was less westernized than the rest.

V5: You had a great deal of success with *THE BLACK DRAGON*, aka *TOUGH GUY*. How did that picture come about?

SK: *AMERICAN TOUGH GUY* was the working title which I later named *THE BLACK DRAGON*. It was my first co-production with Yeo Ban Yee. I wanted to use a black actor as a co-star and not have him killed, since Jim Kelly and Kareem Abdul-Jabbar were both killed in their movies. I proposed the production to Yeo Ban Yee and he accepted my offer. Based on that, I made a second film with him, *THE DEATH OF BRUCE LEE* (1975).

V5: Ron Van Clief made a few more films in the series for them. I take it he had a good experience with Yang's company?

SK: I made two films with Yeo where I used Ron and he appeared in two other films for Yangtze. Yeo Ban Yee did not interact with the cast very much other than when they were hired. He was an arms-length producer and the two co-productions I made with him, he never appeared on the set once.

V5: How did *THE LAST FIST OF FURY* come about, and the casting of Dragon Lee, and how did it become *THE REAL BRUCE LEE*?

SK: *THE REAL BRUCE LEE* was a series of four B/W films of Bruce Lee when he was a child actor. After his death, it was important to showcase his early films, to see the acting experience he had, but the audience, though interested, wanted to see action and Bruce Li and Dragon Lee provided the action.

V5: Did you meet either Bruce Li or Bruce Le?

SK: No, though I did distribute films starring Bruce Le.

V5: What was your opinion of the Bruce Lee imitators then, and your opinion of them now?

SK: There was no one who could imitate Bruce Lee. The look-alikes did not look like Bruce Lee, act like him, or perform and fight like him. They were acceptable at the time, since there was no other option, but today they would not be considered to be used as imitators. There's one maybe two other actors who are much better fighters than Bruce Li and Le, but they would also not be able to pull off being a good Bruce Lee imitator.

Fifty years after Lee's passing, controversy surrounding his life and mystery hovering over his death remain. There are only three people with the answers to both and two of them are dead; those three being Betty Ting Pei, Raymond Chow (died November 2nd, 2018), and Bruce Lee (died July 20th, 1973).

Looking back at the Bruceploitation movement, it was a sub-genre that was widely mocked by critics and largely rejected by the local audience. For occidental viewers, the films were akin to the Carnival Sideshow where the allure of seeing human oddities was hard to resist. The spirit of Bruce Lee and his short but successful life looms large over the men that copied him; and the movies that were less about keeping the man's name alive than making a fast dollar off of it. Regardless, the evolution of the Bruce Imitator phase was a distinctive time in HK film history that cannot be captured again. It began and remains a contentious and divisive subject that fans can relive, love, hate, and debate for years to come.

If you'd like to purchase a copy of Serafilm Karalexis's 2023 book, 'How To Produce a Low Budget Film (Without Any of Your Money)', you can do so at Amazon or directly from Bear Manor Media.

FANATICAL DRAGON REVIEWS

THE GAME OF CLONES
BRUCEPLOITATION COLLECTION VOL.1

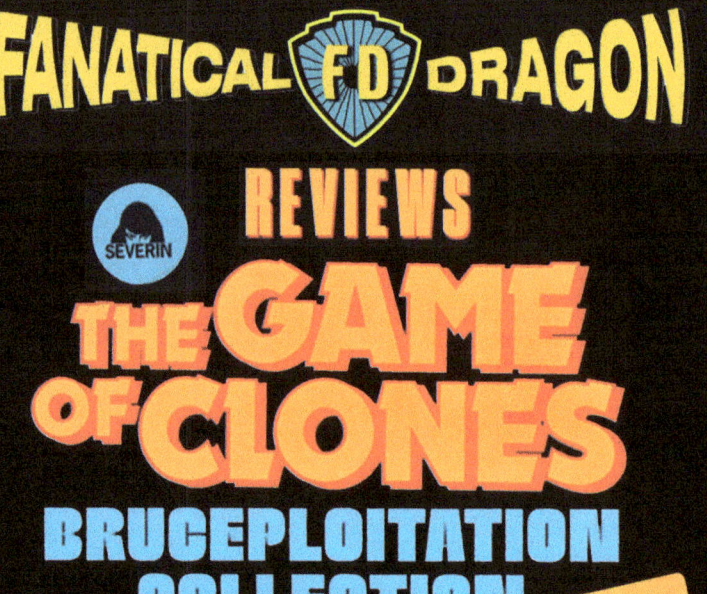

In a year absolutely packed to the bursting point with extremely impressive physical media releases of East Asian Cinema old and new, very few releases have created quite as much of an impact as Severin Films Game of Clones Boxset (Volume 1) and the feature length documentary which effectively inspired it's creation, Enter The Clones Of Bruce. together they represent a triumphant celebration of all things Bruceploitation and whether you love or hate that these movies exist, nobody can deny the incredible work that Severin's David Gregory along with Producer and Bruceploitation expert Michael Worth and The Master of Remaster himself, Frank Djeng have been able to assemble here. Having had the set in my hands for almost a month, I have just about finished working my way through the box, it's been a hell of a fun journey experiencing the movies that Severin have included and the wealth of bonus materials they have created to help showcase this particularly insane period of HK martial Arts cinema. Join me as I dive back into the set once more and try my best to help showcase what will be for many kung fu fans, THE best release of 2024.

PLEASE NOTE - I ordered the boxset direct from Severin which is currently the only way to obtain the webstore only bonus disc, which includes two of what have been amongst the rarest Bruceploitation movies to track down, the Big Boss Part 2 and the Black Dragon Vs the Yellow Tiger.
Let's work though the set disc by disc…

By Johnny Burnett aka *The Fanatical Dragon*

8 DISCS ✱ 15 FILMS ✱ 24+ HOURS OF SPECIAL FEATURES

INCLUDES THE AWARD-WINNING DOCUMENTARY Enter The Clones Of BRUCE

DISC ONE
THE DOCUMENTARY

It's very fitting that the first disc in the box is dedicated to the feature length documentary Enter The Clones of Bruce, It sets the tone for what will follow when you get to the films and also really places the entire sub genre of Bruceploitation into context of where HK cinema was at in the early 70's after Bruce Lee's untimely passing. It also manages to achieve much much more by expanding it's scope out to really examine Martial Arts Cinema in general, with a 10 min section dedicated to Shaw Brothers as well taking steps to examine the issues with archival and restoration of movies form this period. The list of interviewees that Gregory, Worth and Djeng have been able to assemble here is incredible and often significantly poignant as several of the figures interviewed here have since passed away, in the case of the wonderful Philip Ko Fei, this was his very last interview before his passing. it's a real treat to see him speaking here with such conviction and enthusiasm. We also get interviews with Sammo Hung, David Chiang, Angela Mao, Godfrey Ho, Mars, Eric Tseng, Lee Tso-Nam, Yusuaki Kurata and Lo Meng amongst a host of others.. Of course the big draw for the film are the main Bruce Lee 'Clones' that were tasked with the arguably impossible job of filling the void left behind by Bruce's Passing and the documentary forms it's beating heart around the four main 'Clones' that they

Enter The Clones Of BRUCE
FRANK DJENG INTERVIEW

The Fanatical Dragon — Frank Djeng, ENTER THE CLONES OF BRUCE

Enter The Clones Of BRUCE
MICHAEL WORTH INTERVIEW

were able to meet and speak with, Bruce Li, Bruce Le, Bruce Liang and Dragon Lee are all given a chance to really explain their own perspective and experiences on being asked

to follow in Lee's footsteps. Director (and Severin films Co-Owner) David Gregory does a masterful job of assembling the film, I was familiar with his Documentary work already having already seen his wonderful film *LOST SOUL: THE DOOMED JOURNEY OF RICHARD STANLEY'S ISLAND OF DR. MOREAU* which really dives deep into showcasing how insane the production of that movie was and how difficult a period for original director Richard Stanley, so i was really excited to see how he would handle a whole sub genre rather than just being laser focused in on one single movie. His work here is extremely impressive, the documentary flows extremely well. the runtime has been cut down from it's original assembly edit length of 3 hours to 94mins, but thankfully almost all the footage cut out has been presented alongside the main documentary in the form of bonus features.

The full list of bonus features for the documentary is extensive and as mentioned above, offer up almost all the footage shot over the course of several years for the project...

Enter The Clones Special Features:

• Audio Commentary With Co-Executive Producer/Director David Gregory, Co-Producers Frank Djeng, Vivian Wong And Michael Worth And Director Of Photography Jim Kunz
• Working At Shaw Brothers – Outtakes With Godfrey Ho, David Chiang, Yasuaki Kurata, Lee Chiu, Lo Meng, Mars And Phillip Ko
• Bruce Lee And I – Outtakes With Sammo Hung, Phillip Ko, Yasuaki Kurata, Mars, Angela Mao, Andre Morgan, Lee Tso Nam And More
• The Lost World Of Kung Fu Film Negatives – Outtakes With Godfrey Ho, Joseph Lai, Angela Mao, Lee Tso Nam And Film Preservationists
• Bruce's Hong Kong – Location Tour With Frank Djeng
• Severin's Kung Fu Theater With Actor/Director/Bruceploitation Expert Michael Worth
• Trailers

If you're on the fence about making the commitment to buying the whole boxset, then i implore you to at least pick up the standalone release of the documentary, it's available on DVD, Bluray and as a digital streaming option as well as now being available to view on Amazon Prime. It's essential viewing for ALL fans of Martial Arts Cinema not just those interested in Bruceploitation movies...

I would argue that that last sentence rings true for the movies themselves too, I love

Bruce Lee, I adore his movies but given his tragic passing the truth remains that he only had a chance to make 4 fully completed films (Game of Death is essentially a straight up Bruceploitation film in the very truest sense) there were hundreds of independent Bruceploitation movies that his passing inspired, some of them are very bad, some are extremely good and some are just plain weird. the films included in the boxset showcase a great sampling of just how diverse and varied that sub genre would ultimately become.

So lets move onto the films actually included in this first Game of Clones Volume (Severin have already confirmed a second volume is in the works for release later this year or into 2025)

THE MOVIES

Disc 2:
THE CLONES OF BRUCE LEE (1980)
Runtime: 90 mins
English Mono / Closed Captions
Region Free
Aspect Ratio: 2.40:1

Kicking things off we get the Clones Of Bruce Lee, a delightfully insane Sci-Fi/ Kung Fu mashup of a movie and a great first entry in the Boxset for Bruce Le and Dragon Lee, two of the more skilled Martial Artists amongst the various actors who were involved in the sub genre over the years. It's from 1980,

some six years or so into the explosion of Bruceploitation flicks, and presents a much more campy Sci-Fi plot than many of the earlier straight up Biopic style films offered up.

Jon T Benn's Professor Lucas is tasked with cloning Bruce lee after his passing and creates three 'identical' Bruce Lee Clones played here by Bruce Le, Dragon Le and Bruce Lai. Our three new Bruce's are trained up by Bolo Yeung and (Shaw Brothers veteran) The incredible Chiang Tao After the Bruce's are dispatched on various assignments, Bruce #1 is sent undercover to work as an actor and take down a corrupt producer whilst Bruce's #2 & #3 are sent to Thailand to stop a Mad Scientist in his plans for World Domination. After completing their missions and returning back to HK, A disgruntled Professor Lucas ends up attempting to pit them against each other, which after a few back and forth sparring matches fails and the Clones rise up against their creator to bring him to justice. It's all somewhat campy and very cheesy but still extremely good fun and the fighting sequences are the draw here, especially Bruce Le and Dragon Lee. Chiang Tao also proves himself extremely adept at a more comedic role than he was often afforded during his time at Shaw's. it's a excellent first movie to kick things off with and it's no surprise it's been given the bulk of the special features over Enter Three Dragons.. Each film on the set includes an Introduction from Michael Worth, these are great, short little films where Michael gets to run through the basic setup for each movie and explain where they were able to source the movie form and the state each film was in when they found it.We also get a great interview with Jon T Benn and a wonderful Audio Commentary with Micheal Worth and Frank Djeng joined by a host of guests..

Special Features:
• Audio Commentary With Michael Worth And Frank Djeng, Co-Producers Of ENTER THE CLONES OF BRUCE; Bruce Lee Historian Brandon Bentley; Chris Poggiali, Co-Author Of These Fists Break Bricks; Matthew Whitaker, Co-Host Of The Clones Cast; Action Film Historian Mike Leeder; Stunt Coordinator/Author John Kreng; And Rick Benn, Brother Of Actor Jon T. Benn
• The Big Boss Remembered – Interview With Actor Jon T. Benn
• Severin's Kung Fu Theater With Actor/ Director/Bruceploitation Expert Michael Worth • Trailer

ENTER THREE DRAGONS (1978)

Runtime: 87 mins
English Mono / Closed Captions
Region Free
Aspect Ratio: 2.35:1

The second film on disc two is a more erratic and often slightly confusing affair, 1978's Enter Three Dragons features Dragon Lee in his first HK movie role, a paper thin plot of a young man named Sammy (played by Samuel Wells) falling foul of gangsters after he loses a batch of diamonds and then his friends Bruce and Dragon Hong are pulled into the fray when they try to help him out. His two friends here being played by Bruce Lai and Dragon Lee, though Bruce is playing Dragon and Dragon is playing Bruce. Told you it was confusing, and that's just the casting. None of this really matters though, the action is extremely entertaining, the English dub is hilarious and endlessly quotable and there are some great supporting performances from Shaw's regulars Philip Ko and Lee Hoi-Sang (it's astounding how often Lee Hoi-Sang crops up in the last act of these movies often just for one single sequence) Michael Worth gives us a great introduction for the piece alongside a trailer…

Special Features:
• Severin's Kung Fu Theater With Actor/Director/ Bruceploitation Expert Michael Worth
• Trailer

Disc 3:
ENTER THE GAME OF DEATH (1978)

Runtime: 90 mins
English Mono / Closed Captions
Region Free
Aspect Ratio: 2.35:1

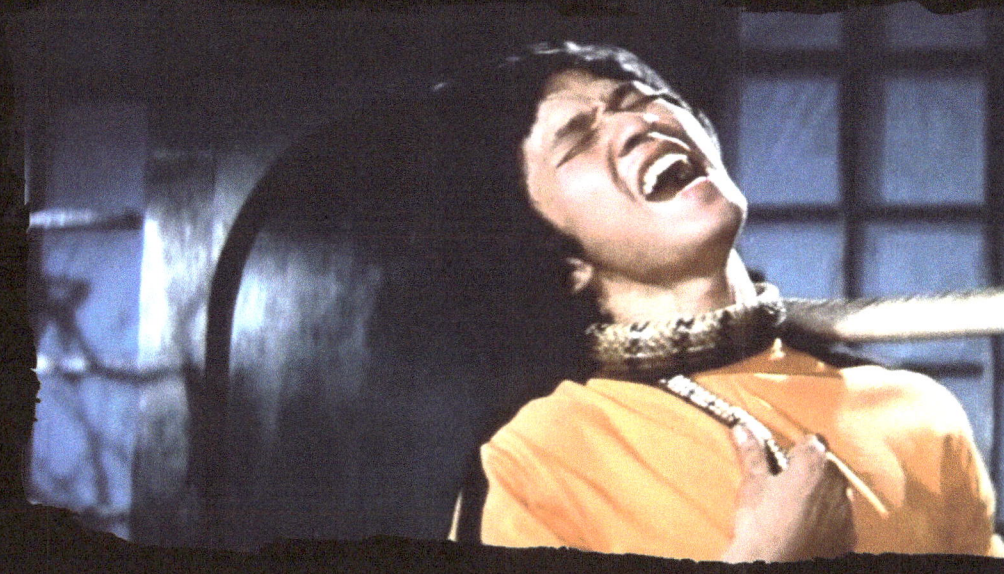

Disc three delivers one of my favourite Bruceploitation flicks, 1978's Enter The Game Of Death starring Bruce Le, mostly as i'm a huge fan of Director Lee Tso-Nam, and whilst this may not be one of his strongest directorial entries, it's still a entertaining movie that riffs on the original Game Of Death / Tower of Death concept. Bruce Le's Mr Ang is coaxed into helping an undercover

Chinese agent working for the Japanese to enter into a Tower of Death and fight his way to the top of the tower to retrieve an important 'document'. As is often the case in these movies plot is secondary to action and in this case, to allow our hero to go toe to toe against a variety of different villains each sporting different techniques/gimmick. Once again the mighty Lee Hoi-San comes in for a one time boss fight as does the wonderful Chi Ling Chiu who features pretty extensively in the special features on the disc. In the light of all 2 hours of Bruce Lee's original Game of Death footage surfacing last year and being featured on Arrow Video's boxset, some of the beats in this movie feel oddly clairvoyant, as when Enter The Game of Death was made, I'm doubtful they had access to Bruce Lee's footage or his notes for his intended plans. But several moments here are uncannily similar to what Lee had hoped to deliver had he been able to finish the project (though

obviously, likely to a much slicker and more sophisticated degree) most notably in the 'red light' room used on one floor of the pagoda. All in all though, it's one of the best Bruce Le movies on this set for me, there was previously a Bluray release out of Germany from The Vengeance Pack, but the version on Severin's set looks like they've worked from a nicer print.

Special Features:
• Partial Audio Commentary With Actor/Director/Bruceploitation Expert Michael Worth
• Scene Specific Commentary With Actor Chi Ling Chiu
• Kung Fu Movie Hustle – Interview With Chi Ling Chiu
• Talking A Good Game – Roundtable Discussion With Martial Artists/Kung Fu Film Experts Tatevik Hunanyan, John Kreng, Ron Strong And Michael Worth
• Severin's Kung Fu Theater With Michael Worth
• Trailer

GOODBYE, BRUCE LEE: HIS LAST GAME OF DEATH (1975)

Runtime: 83 mins
English Mono / Closed Captions
Region Free
Aspect Ratio: 2.35:1

The other 'Tower of Death' movie included on Disc 3 is 1975's Goodbye, Bruce Lee: His Last Game of Death, the first Bruce Li movie on the set and one of the contenders for best soundtrack on the movie, the theme song King Of Kung Fy bu Candy gets most of the praise, but there are also some other pretty cool needle drops (Also Sprach Zarathustra by Strauss - the opening theme from Stanley Kubrick's 2001 A Space Odyssey is used several times) The film is a quite meta mix of real life events (Bruce Lee's passing and the desire to find a new actor to follow in his footsteps) but the movie that our hero is being hired to work on, inside the movie, also stars Bruce Li, they frequently mix video and stills of the real Bruce Lee alongside Bruce Li. There is a sub plot in the movie within the movie about a criminal tricking Bruce Li into delivering a

It's also a pretty great Pagoda location, we get a bunch of shots from outside shooting up at the fighters sparring outside the top floor and some shots of Bruce being forced against the barrier on one of the higher levels showing just how high up they were filming. All in all it's a pretty solid fun movie back up by another great set of extras included. Michael Worth & Frank Djeng's the Last Kung Fu Picture Show short film being particularly notable. The two speak about the various cinemas in the San Francisco area where they recall watching key movies, Michael in particular has a long, long history with watching Bruceploitation movies in the various locations they showcase. It's a heartfelt and really interesting extra.

package for him to gangsters which escalates over the course of the movie to the goons kidnapping Bruce's girlfriend and holding her hostage in the Tower of Death. He then has to don the old yellow jumpsuit and fight his way up the tower level by level. Maybe not quite as dramatically filmed as Enter The Game of Death and the fighters he meets are generally less colourful than those we saw in Bruce Le's movie, but it's more grounded and as such carries a little more dramatic weight to it, this is helped by Bruce Li being arguably the best actor of the various Clones and he also does his best to sell the emotions and situations with some depth and resonance.

Special Features:
• Audio Commentary With Frank Djeng, Co-Producer Of ENTER THE CLONES OF BRUCE, With Contributions From Chris Poggiali, Co-Author Of These Fists Break Bricks
• The Last Kung Fu Picture Show – The Bay Area's Movie Theater Era
• Severin's Kung Fu Theater With Actor/Director/Bruceploitation Expert Michael Worth
• Radio Spot
• Trailer

Disc 4:
THE DRAGON LIVES AGAIN (1977)

Runtime: 91 mins
English Mono / Closed Captions
Region Free
Aspect Ratio: 2.39:1

Potentially taking the title of maddest movie included in the volume, 1977's The Dragon Lives Again is an utterly insane journey into the underworld as we watch Bruce Liang resurrect in the afterlife and have to contend with fending off the the King of The Underworld's horny wives, Count Dracula and his army of skeletal and mummy style zombies, Clint Eastwood, James Bond and Zatoichi all here acting as low level gang thugs and his only allies are Popeye, The One Armed Swordsman and Caine from Kung Fu. It's a hell of a lot of fun, there is ample nudity courtesy of the King's wives and a random Emanuelle parody but there is also a significant amount of pretty great choreography from Bruce Liang and a whole lot of laughs. I can see this one being one of the most popular titles on the set actually, it's a perfect match for watching with a bunch of mates and a significant amount of alcohol.

Special Features:
• Audio Commentary With Michael Worth And Frank Djeng, Co-Producers Of ENTER THE CLONES OF BRUCE
• Deleted Scenes From French Version
• Audio Essay By Cult Cinema Critic Lovely Jon
• Severin's Kung Fu Theater With Actor/Director/Bruceploitation Expert Michael Worth
• Trailer

BRUCE AND THE IRON FINGER (1979)

Runtime: 89 mins
English Mono / Closed Captions
Region Free
Aspect Ratio: 2.39:1

We're on much more sombre and for me, more interesting territory with Bruce and the Iron Finger, playing out like a police procedural / serial killer murder mystery. With Bruce Li going undercover in a Kung Fu School to try and track down a killer who has been dispatching various Martial Artists around the city using a deadly Iron Finger Technique. the Avenging Eagle villain himself Ku Feng is on great form here as the Iron Fingered villain and we get to once more see Lee Hoi-San doing his turn up for one sequence thing (sporting a great captains hat and white shirt combo) You can see Bruce Li's development as an actor as he's already progressed quite far from his work in Goodbye Bruce Lee and the action is better realised with more of a street brawl style to it with far far less nods to Bruce Lee's various trademarks moves and the movie is all the better for it.

Special Features:
• Audio Commentary With Actor/Director/Bruceploitation Expert Michael Worth
• My First Bruceploitation – Roundtable Discussion With Martial Artists/Kung Fu Film Experts Tatevik Hunanyan, John Kreng, Ron Strong And Michael Worth
• Deleted Scenes
• Severin's Kung Fu Theater With Michael Worth
• U.S. Trailer
• Hong Kong Trailer

Disc 5:
CHALLENGE OF THE TIGER (1980)

Runtime: 89 mins
English Mono / Closed Captions
Region Free
Aspect Ratio: 2.35:1

Challenge of the Tiger was one of the real surprise hits of the set for me, I'd not seen it before picking up the boxset and it ended up being one of the movies i enjoyed the most. It's also one of the least Bruceploitation-esque movies on offer here, it's basically more of a martial arts/action movie that just happens to star Bruce Le (who also co-wrote and directed the movie) The plot revolves around the search for a scientific formula that has the power to make men infertile which is stolen in the opening minutes of the movie. Bruce Le and Richard Harrison are tasked with retrieving the sperm busting MacGuffin in this spy thriller style romp set partly in Spain and then moving to Hong Kong. Excellent supporting roles for Chiang Tao and Hwang Jang-Lee and a brief cameo from Bolo Yeung. Bruce Le gets to go up against a (rather skinny) Bull, some motorbike riding thugs and a whole bunch of goons over the course of the movie and his choreography here is faster, more brutal and much better realised than many of his earlier movies. Richard Harrison doesn't get much to do aside from bedding several girls over the course of the film. but he makes for a pretty good sidekick to our main hero.

Special Features:
• Audio Commentary With Actor/Director/Bruceploitation Expert Michael Worth And Film Historian C. Courtney Joyner
• Severin's Kung Fu Theater With Michael Worth
• Trailer

CAMEROON CONNECTION (1984)

Runtime: 91 mins
French Mono / English Subtitles
Region Free
Aspect Ratio: 2.35:1

This one was a bit of a misfire for me, very much of a vanity project for Director/Star Alphonse Beni who plays a Police officer trying to solve the case of a murdered girl. Bruce Le isn't in it that much, but the film definitely picks up when he is. I enjoyed the 50min Lights.Cameroon…Action! special feature more than the main movie, it was a great retrospective look at Alphonse Beni's life and work and was arguably far better made than the film it supports.

Special Features:
• Audio Commentary With Writer/Criterion Reflections Podcast Host David Blakeslee
• Lights... Cameroon... Action! – The Life And Films Of Alphonse Beni
• 2022 Q&A With Alphonse Beni At Cine Club N'Kah
 • Severin's Kung Fu Theater With Actor/Director/Bruceploitation Expert Michael Worth

Disc 6:
SUPER DRAGON: THE BRUCE LEE STORY (1974)

Runtime: 93 mins
English Mono / Closed Captions
Region Free
Aspect Ratio: 2.35:1

Disc Six delivers the two Bruce Lee biopics on the set, both starring Bruce Li. 1974's Super Dragon is a more melodramatic affair, light on action, but it does offer a good indication of how much Bruce Li's acting progressed between the two Biopic movies presented on the disc. I tend to prefer the more outlandish and more action packed entires in the genre, so wasn't as engaged with Super Dragon as I was with other entries in the boxset. but I'm sure there will be those of you out there that are much more drawn to these specifically for their portrayal of some of the more grounded events lifted from Bruce Lee's life.

Special Features:
• Partial Audio Commentary With Actor/Director/Bruceploitation Expert Michael Worth
• Severin's Kung Fu Theater With Michael Worth
• TV Spot
• Trailer

THE DRAGON LIVES (1976)

Runtime: 87 mins
English Mono / Closed Captions
Region Free
Aspect Ratio: 2.39:1

This was the better of the two biopics on the disc, the Dragon Lives from 1976. It's one of the only Bruce Lee biopics to cover his whole life from birth to death and whilst they have taken some weird liberties in places. it's a much more interesting and balanced movie than Super Dragon. Bruce Li is also markedly better here as he continued to hone his craft. Unsurprisingly, way more extras have been offered up for The Dragon Lives, the interview with Caryn White Stedman is especially good, she plays Linda Lee in the movie and her recollections of the production were very interesting to listen back to.

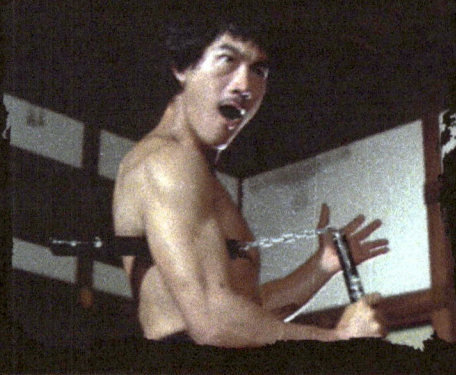

Special Features:
• Audio Commentary With Actress Caryn White Stedman And Actor/Director/Bruceploitation Expert Michael Worth
• Audio Interview With "He's A Legend, He's

"A Hero" Songwriter Anders Gustav Nelsson
• The Taiwan Connection – Interview With Caryn White Stedman
• Bruce Biopics – Roundtable Discussion With Martial Artists/Kung Fu Film Experts Tatevik Hunanyan, John Kreng, Ron Strong And Michael Worth
• Severin's Kung Fu Theater With Michael Worth
• TV Spots

Disc 7:
THE DRAGON, THE HERO (1980)
Runtime: 87 mins
English Mono / Closed Captions
Region Free
Aspect Ratio: 2.35:1

We're back on more action packed footing for Disc 7, and actually very foot work based

as we kick off with Godfrey Ho's the Dragon, The Hero, starring Dragon Lee though here in a little more of a supporting role to John Liu. Philip Ko Fei gets another great turn as a villain and we even get another Bolo cameo, here playing a hairy chested (and feet) strong man. It's a much more shapes based, traditional style Kung Fu flick, and one of the Godfrey Ho's most entertaining Martial Arts pictures that he actually shot every part of (no cut and paste style work on display here a la Ninja Terminator) A great cadre of pretty colourful villains, including a intriguing Wheelchair bound mastermind with a make up job that channels Tommy Lee in The Hot, The Cool and The Vicious. The Bonus feature interview with Godfrey Ho is absolutely fantastic, his presence on the set is a real joy, he also joins Michael Worth for a commentary track for the movie. Excellent stuff.

Special Features:
• Audio Commentary With Director Godfrey Ho And Actor/Director/Bruceploitation Expert Michael Worth
• Godfrey, The Hero – Interview With Director Godfrey Ho
• Deleted Scenes
• Severin's Kung Fu Theater With Michael Worth
• Trailer

RAGE OF THE DRAGON (1980)
Runtime: 90 mins
English Mono / Closed Captions
Region Free
Aspect Ratio: 2.35:1

The second feature on Disc 7 is a much more effective vehicle for Dragon Lee than The Dragon, Then Hero, he really gets to take the lead here in one of the best straight up Kung Fu flicks on the set. It's very much like a Korean take on the Yuen Woo Ping style. There are still some of Dragon's Bruce Lee mannerisms on show here, but also a much more explosive animal form style of choreography and a pretty great villain performance from Carter Wong as a light

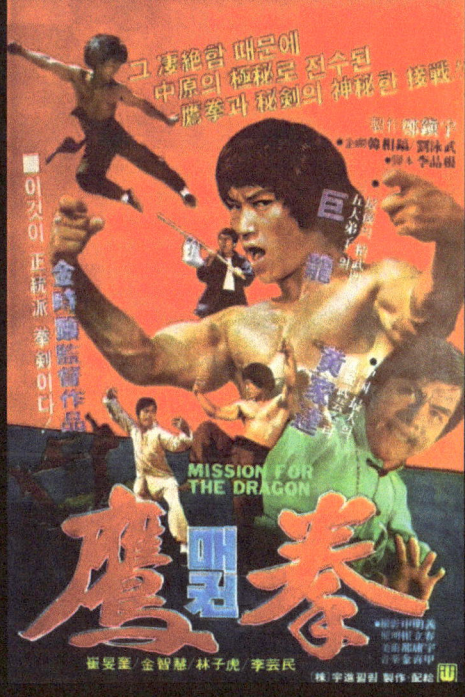

sensitive, scheming, red ninja leading heavy. The finale where Dragon Lee employs a vest made of mirrors to defeat Wong is one of the standout fights in the movies included.

Special Features:
• Audio Commentary With Actor/Director/Bruceploitation Expert Michael Worth With Contributions From Chris Poggiali, Co-Author Of These Fists Break Bricks
• Kung Fu Theaters – Roundtable Discussion With Martial Artists/Kung Fu Film Experts Tatevik Hunanyan, John Kreng, Ron Strong And Michael Worth
• Severin's Kung Fu Theater With Michael Worth
• Trailer

Disc 8 (Webstore Exclusive Limited Edition Bonus Disc):
THE BIG BOSS PART II (1976)
Runtime: 91 mins
Mandarin Mono / Burned-In English Subtitles, Burned-In Chinese Subtitles
Region Free
Aspect Ratio: 2.39:1

This 1976 unofficial sequel to Lee's original was almost mythical due to its rarity and Severin have finally brought it to home video including it in the boxset via a webstore exclusive disc. Here Bruce Le takes on Lee's role of Cheng Chao-en alongside the wonderful Lo Lieh who plays Cheng's brother. Chan Chue, who

played the The ice house manager from the original movie returns to star here and also directs the film. We also return to many of the locations used in the Bruce Lee original. This is much more of a straight up revenge flick and Lo Lieh is always entertaining to watch, especially when playing more heroic characters, which he so rarely got a chance to do at Shaw Brothers who tended to utilise him far more often for Villainous characters. This is the only movie on this volume in

Mandarin (with burned in English Subtitles)

Special Features:
• Severin's Kung Fu Theater With Actor/Director/Bruceploitation Expert Michael Worth
• Trailer

THE BLACK DRAGON VS. THE YELLOW TIGER (1974)

Runtime: 88 mins
English Mono / Closed Captions
Region Free
Aspect Ratio: 2.39:1

The other movie included on the bonus disc is also a semi-sequel, this time to Way Of the Dragon, Tong Lung, one of the lesser seen Bruce Clones steps up for the lead, which sees gangsters from a group calling themselves The Black Hand gunning for Bruce Lee after he refuses to throw a fight and end up mistaking Tong Lung for the man himself and going after him instead.. It's not the best movie on the set by a long shot, but an interesting entry as it's one of the earliest on offer here. This Taiwanese movie actually went into production when Bruce Lee was still alive. American Martial Artist Clint Robinson ends up being the final fighter that Tong Lung faces off against and he contributes to the audio commentary.

Special Features:
• Audio Commentary With Actor/Director/Bruceploitation Expert Michael Worth With Contributions From Actor Clint Robinson
• Severin's Kung Fu Theater With Michael Worth
• Trailer

The Movie discs are all housed inside a really nice folding book style case with info and sit nicely alongside the excellent 100page book. Design and layout for the book is by Ken Miller and works really well in capturing the tone and feel of many of the posters of the movies and the era. Alongside a wealth of images from the movies their marketing materials we also get several really well written articles from Michael Worth, Chris Poggiali, Roger Cross and Jon Casbard examining the sub genre, the Bruce Clones and their impact into America in the 70's and 80's and the rise of Ocean Shore and Continental Pictures. All in all its a really well presented and really informative companion to the movies and the on disc extras.

And that's Volume1 - I'm extremely excited to see what titles Severin have up their sleeves for us all in Volume 2, Severin have really delivered above and beyond with the boxset, it's a spectacular achievement for an all too often much maligned sub genre of East Asian Cinema. Here the movies have been treated with an enormous amount of respect, admiration and enthusiasm.
And in many cases, have never, and will never, look this good anywhere else!

If you are keen for more Game of Clones related content, please jump over to my Youtube channel and check out the long form interviews I've conducted recently with Frank Djeng and Michael Worth, both speak at length about the boxset and the Enter The Clones documentary and Michael Worth's sharing his extensive knowledge on Bruceploitation is a real joy to listen to. You can find both interviews by checking out my channel at:

www.youtube.com/thefanaticaldragon
WRITTEN BY JOHNNY BURNETT AKA
THE FANATICAL DRAGON

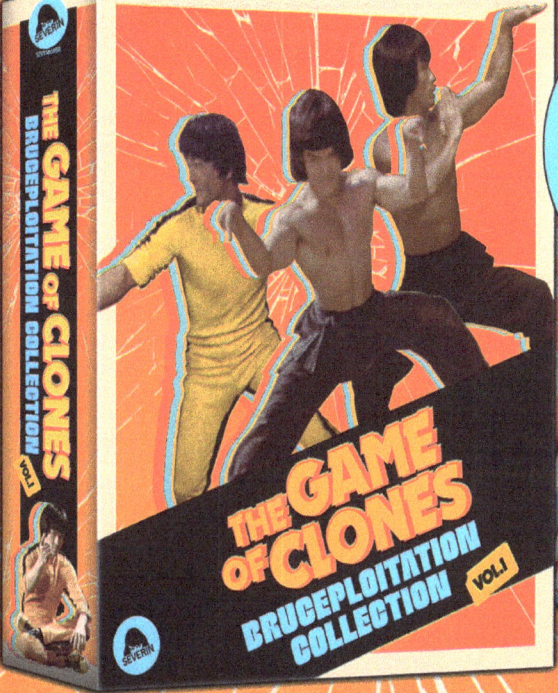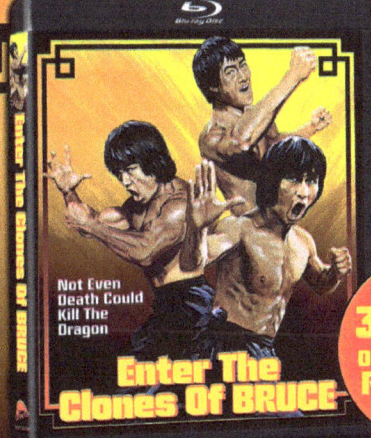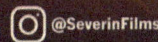

COLLECTING BRUCE LEE LPs

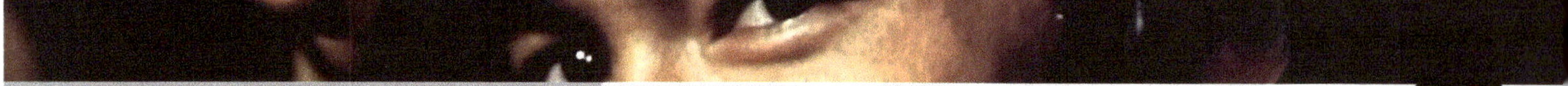

By Michael Nesbitt

In the final instalment of the Bruce Lee vinyl record collection of articles, we take a close look at various 12 inch LPs relating to Bruce Lee that were released during the 1970s and 80s. Out of all the vinyl's we have covered, Bruce Lee LPs, are by far the more collectible, especially the Japanese LPs. Considering CDs replaced LPs as far back at the mid-1980s, collectors will still pay well over £100 for certain rare LPs that they want to add to their collection. Like most genres in the vinyl collection, the Japanese market was far superior in their releases, with well over 100 relating to Bruce Lee. Some of these releases were built up of compilation LPs, soundtracks from different movies that were popular at the time. Here we show the ones that have Bruce Lee, either on the front or back cover. The others where he is pictured inside, we have left out of the article, we have just focused on the main LPs due to lack of space. We have also added a few LP records from the European and American markets; these are more easily attainable, but just as collectible.

When collecting Japanese LPs, it is important to try and purchase the ones that still have the OBI attached. OBI's were a paper band or a folded paper flap that was attached to each LP. These OBI's, were all written in Japanese, and would give highlighted information of what was included in and on the record. These were normally found on imported LPs that had the text written in English. However, OBI's started to appear on most Japanese released LPs, especially if they came with a free poster, which would be highlighted on the OBI itself along with the other information. Some Japanese records didn't come with an OBI, these were records that came from boxsets, compiled of various albums.

(Please note, all these albums come from my private collection, and some of the rarer ones pictured, don't have their OBI attached. Each record which came with an OBI will be mentioned in the information section, even if it is not seen in the photo).

Title: The Green Hornet - Theme from TVs Hottest New Hero
Year: 1966
Country: USA
Label: Coronet Records
Side A: 5 Tracks
Side B: 5 Tracks
Info: A compilation of music from the 1966 Green Hornet TV Series, including the main theme tune 'Flight of the Bumble Bee'.

Title: The Horn Meets the Hornet
Year: 1966
Country: USA
Label: RCA
Side A: 6 Tracks
Side B: 5 Tracks
Info: The Green Hornet music by Al (He's The King) Hirt. Also includes music from classic TV shows such as The Monkeys, Run Buddy Run, Tarzan, Batman and others. This album doesn't have Bruce Lee on the cover, but it does have Van Williams as the 1966 Green Hornet on the front.

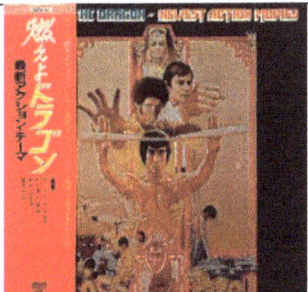

Title: Enter The Dragon - Newest Action Movies
Year: 1973
Country: Japan
Label: CBS/Sony
Side A: 6 Tracks
Side B: 6 Tracks
Info: A compilation album with music from Enter the Dragon, Shaft, Super Fly, The Godfather and others. Includes OBI, 1 x LP, Gatefold with no inserts.

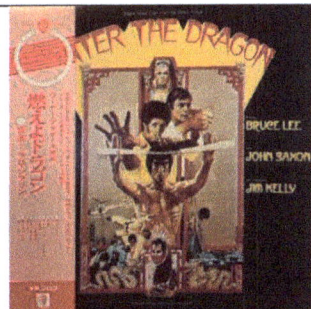

Title: Enter The Dragon
Year: 1973
Country: Japan
Label: Warner Brothers Records
Side A: 5 Tracks
Side B: 5 Tracks
Info: The original soundtrack from the motion picture by Lalo Schifrin. This original Japanese pressing for Enter the Dragon is the same as the American release. Includes OBI and 1 insert.

Title: The Green Hornet
Year: 1974
Country: USA
Label: Mark 56 Records
Side A: The Hornet Does It
Side B: Bootleg Printing Scheme
Info: Two Complete episodes of the Green Hornet Radio Show, which was first broadcast on Detroit's WXYZ Radio Channel in 1936.

Title: Action and Spectacle Movie Themes
Year: 1974
Country: Japan
Label: CBS-Sony
LP 1, A: 6 Tracks. **B**: 6 Tracks
LP 2, A: 6 Tracks. **B**: 6 Tracks
Info: A compilation album, with music from; Fist of Fury, Enter the Dragon, The Longest Day, The Great Escape, Ben Hur, A Fist Full of Dollars, The Magnificent Seven and others. This is a box set of 3 x LPs. Includes OBI and 1 insert.

Title: Bruce Lee in Fist Of Fury
Year: 1974
Country: Japan
Label: Tam
Side A: 6 Tracks
Side B: 4 Tracks
Info: The original soundtrack by Joseph Koo and Ku Chia Hui from Fist of Fury. The first release version came with a pre-printed signed photo of Bruce from Fist of Fury. This wasn't included in the re-release.

Title: Great Action Film Themes
Year: 1974
Country: UK
Label: Sunset Records
Side A: 6 Tracks
Side B: 6 Tracks
Info: A compilation album, with theme music from Enter the Dragon, Fist of Fury, James Bond, The French Connection and Shaft, plus others.

Title: Screen Music Deluxe
Year: 1974
Country: Japan
Label: Seven Seas
LP 1, A: 6 Tracks. **B**: 6 Tracks
LP 2, A: 6 Tracks. **B**: 6 Tracks
Info: A compilation album which included music from; My Fair Lady, Enter the Dragon, plus others. 3 x Vinyl, Gatefold. Includes 1 insert.

Title: The Best Collection of Movie Themes 7 - Suspense
Year: 1974
Country: Japan
Label: CBS-Sony
LP 1, A: 6 Tracks. **B**: 6 Tracks
LP 2, A: 6 Tracks. **B**: 6 Tracks
Info: A compilation album, with music from; Airport, Earthquake, Charade, Bonnie and Clyde, Enter the Dragon and others. 2 x LPs, Gatefold, no insert.

Title: The Big Boss
Year: 1974
Country: Japan
Label: Tam
Side A: 5 Tracks
Side B: 5 Tracks
Info: The original soundtrack for the Big Boss by Joseph Koo and Wang Fu Ling. Comes with an OBI and a large Hong Kong movie poster of The Big Boss.

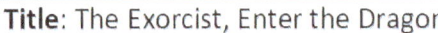

Title: The Exorcist, Enter the Dragon
Year: 1974
Country: Japan
Label: Warner Brothers Records
LP 1, A: 6 Tracks. **B**: 6 Tracks
LP 2, A: 6 Tracks. **B**: 6 Tracks
Info: A compilation album which includes music from; Papillon, Live and Let Die, Great Gatsby, Alfie and many others. 2 x LPs, Gatefold. Comes with an OBI and no insert.

Title: The Greatest Hit Screen Themes
Year: 1974
Country: Japan
Label: Seven Seas/Barclay
Side A: 7 Tracks
Side B: 7 Tracks
Info: A compilation album which includes music from; Enter the Dragon, The Sting, The Exorcist, Papillon and others. Includes an OBI and 1 insert.

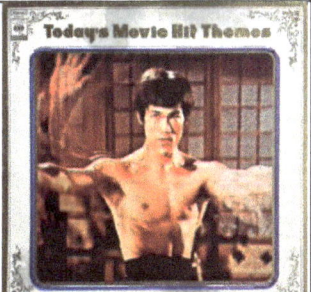

Title: Todays Movie Hit Themes (Wide Deluxe 2500)
Year: 1974
Country: Japan
Label: CBS-Sony
Side A: 8 Tracks
Side B: 7 Tracks
Info: A compilation album, which includes music from; The Entertainer, Enter the Dragon, Fist of Fury, Live and Let Die and others. Comes with an OBI and no inserts.

Title: TV and Movies Big Hits Collection
Year: 1974
Country: Japan
Label: Toho Records
Side A: 5 Tracks
Side B: 6 Tracks
Info: The front of the jacket features the cast of the popular 1970's Japanese T.V. show, Howl at the Sun. Includes themes for Enter the Dragon, Fist of Fury and The Big Boss. Includes an OBI and 1 insert.

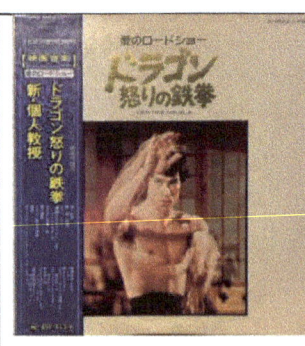	**Title**: Screen Theme Twin Deluxe **Year**: 1974 **Country**: Japan **Label**: Polydor **LP 1, A**: 6 Tracks. **B**: 6 Tracks **LP 2, A**: 6 Tracks. **B**: 6 Tracks **Info**: A compilation album which includes theme music from; Enter the Dragon, The Big Boss, Fist of Fury, Papillon, The Godfather and others. 2 x Vinyl, Gatefold. Comes with an OBI and 1 insert.
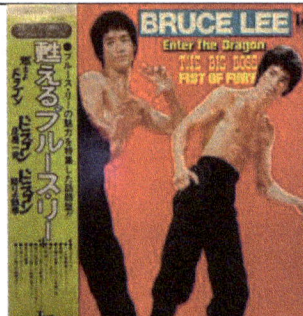	**Title**: Bruce Lee - Enter The Dragon, The Big Boss, Fist Of Fury **Year**: 1974 **Country**: Japan **Label**: Tam **Side A:** 6 Tracks **Side B:** 6 Tracks **Info**: Includes music from Joseph Koo, Wang Fu Ling, Ku Chia Hui. The album has themes from The Big Boss, Fist of Fury and Enter the Dragon. Comes with an OBI and 1 insert.
	**Title**: Action Screen Music Collection (4 Channel) **Year**: 1975 **Country:** Korea **Label**: Philips **Side A**: 6 Tracks **Side B**: 6 Tracks **Info**: A compilation album, with music from; Enter the Dragon, Black Belt Jones, Shanghai Joe, One-Armed Boxer, The Big Boss and others. Includes an OBI and 1 insert.
	Title: Best Action Movies **Year**: 1975 **Country:** Japan **Label**: CBS-Sony **LP 1, A**: 7 Tracks. **B**: 6 Tracks **LP 2, A**: 6 Tracks. **B**: 6 Tracks **Info**: A compilation album which includes theme music from; Godfather part 2, Earthquake, Enter the Dragon, Magnum Force, Shaft, Goldfinger and others. 2 X LPs, Gatefold. Comes with an OBI and no Insert.
	**Title**: Bruce Lee - The Way Of Life **Year**: 1975 **Country:** Japan **Label**: Tam **Side A:** 6 Tracks **Side B**: 6 Tracks **Info**: Music from Joseph Koo and the Stanley Maxfield Orchestra. Comes with an OBI and 1 insert.

	**Title**: Bruce Lee in the Dragon **Year**: 1975 **Country**: Japan **Label**: CBS/Sony **Side A**: 7 Tracks **Side B**: 7 Tracks **Info**: This album included music from The Big Boss, Fist of Fury and Enter the Dragon. All of these were covers performed by the Ensemble Petit & Screenland Orchestra. Includes an OBI and 4 colour calendar prints for 1975.
	**Title**: Dragon Sounds **Year**: 1975 **Country**: Japan **Label**: Warner Brothers Records **Side A**: 6 Tracks **Side B**: 6 Tracks **Info**: A Bruce Lee compilation album, which has music from The Big Boss, Fist of Fury, Way of the Dragon, Enter the Dragon and the Green Hornet. Includes OBI and 1 insert.
	**Title**: Golden 40 - Action Screen Music **Year**: 1975 **Country**: Japan **Label**: Columbia **LP 1, A**: 10 Tracks. **B**: 10 Tracks **LP 2, A**: 10 Tracks. **B**: 10 Tracks **Info**: A compilation album, with music from; Serpico, Getaway, Enter the Dragon, Mission Impossible and others. 2 x Vinyl, Gatefold. Comes with an OBI and no insert.
	**Title**: Golden Screen Themes **Year**: 1975 **Country**: Japan **Label**: Odeon Records **Side A**: 6 Tracks **Side B**: 6 Tracks **Info**: This album came from a boxset of records called Men of Action and Romance. No OBI was issued. Included 1 insert, which is a large booklet giving information on all the albums in the boxset.
	**Title**: Way of the Dragon - Bruce Lee Special **Year**: 1975 **Country**: Japan **Label**: RCA **Side A**: 5 Tracks **Side B**: 5 Tracks **Info**: An album of covers from all of Bruce Lee's movies except Game of Death. Includes OBI, but no inserts.

	**Title**: Screen Action Theme Special **Year**: 1975 **Country**: Japan **Label**: RCA **Side A**: 7 Tracks **Side B**: 7 Tracks **Info**: A compilation album which include music from; The Man with the Golden Gun, Live And Let Die, Enter The Dragon, Airport and others. Includes an OBI and 1 insert.
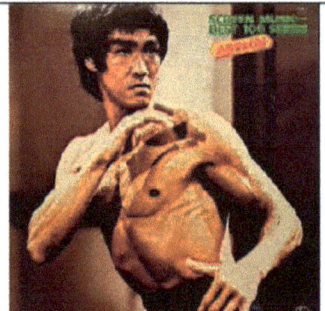	**Title**: Roadshow - Screen Theme Music **Year**: 1975 **Country**: Japan **Label**: Warner Brothers Records **Side A**: 6 Tracks **Side B**: 6 Tracks **Info**: A compilation album which include theme s music from; Emmanuelle, The Man with the Golden Gun, Enter the Dragon and others. Includes an OBI and 1 insert.
	**Title**: Screen Music Best 100 Series – Action **Year**: 1975 **Country**: Japan **Label**: Seven Seas **Side A**: 7 Tracks **Side B**: 7 Tracks **Info**: Themes from Enter the Dragon and The Big Boss. The cover photo was the most used on Japanese LPs, appearing on at least 9 albums. Includes an OBI and 1 insert.
	**Title**: Screen Music Action and Suspense Vol 8 (Big Collection 1500) **Year**: 1975 **Country**: Japan **Label**: Columbia **Side A**: 10 Tracks **Side B**: 10 Tracks **Info**: A compilation album, with music from; James Bond, Earthquake, From Russia with Love, Enter the Dragon, Chinatown and others. Includes an OBI and 1 insert.
	**Title**: Screen Music Action Special **Year**: 1975 **Country**: Japan **Label**: Tam **LP 1, A**: 6 Tracks. **B**: 6 Tracks **LP 2, A**: 6 Tracks. **B**: 6 Tracks **Info**: A compilation album which includes theme music from; Scorpio, Enter the Dragon, The Getaway, Thunderball and others. 2 x LPs, Gatefold. Comes with an OBI and no insert.

 	**Title**: Screen Theme Twin Deluxe **Year**: 1975 **Country**: Japan **Label**: Polydor **LP 1, A**: 6 Tracks. **B**: 6 Tracks **LP 2, A**: 6 Tracks. **B**: 6 Tracks **Info**: A compilation album including music from; The Way of the Dragon, Paper Tiger, Fist of Fury and others. 2 x LPs, Gatefold. Includes a double-sided pull-out poster of Brigitte Bardot and Alain Delon.
	**Title**: The Action Movie Themes (Wide Deluxe 3200) **Year**: 1975 **Country:** Japan **Label**: CBS/Sony **LP 1, A: 6 Tracks. B: 6 Tracks** **LP 2, A: 6 Tracks. B: 6 Tracks** **Info**: A compilation album, which includes music from; Enter the Dragon, Shaft, The Godfather, and others. 2 x LPs, Gatefold. Comes with an OBI and no insert.
	**Title**: The Ballad of Bruce Lee **Year**: 1975 **Country:** USA **Label**: Sunrise **Side A**: 5 Tracks **Side B**: 5 Tracks **Info**: The music from this LP was written and recorded by Robert Lee, Bruce Lee's brother. All the songs on the album are dedicated to Bruce.
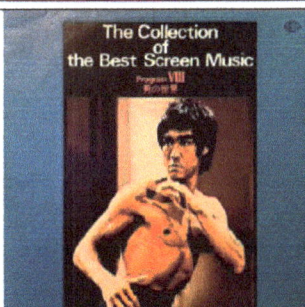	**Title**: The Collection of the Best Screen Music - Volume 8 **Year**: 1975 **Country:** Japan **Label**: Seven Seas **Side A**: 6 Tracks **Side B**: 6 Tracks **Info**: A compilation album with music from; Enter the Dragon, Fist of Fury, Red Sun, Zorba the Greek, The Great Gatsby and others. No OBI or Inserts.
	**Title**: The Great Action Movies **Year**: 1975 **Country:** Japan **Label**: CBS-Sony **LP 1, A: 6 Tracks. B: 6 Tracks** **LP 2, A: 6 Tracks. B: 6 Tracks** **Info**: A compilation album, with music from; Jaws, Zorro, Fist of Fury, Enter the Dragon, The Great Escape and others. 2 x LPs, Gatefold. Comes with an OBI and no inserts.

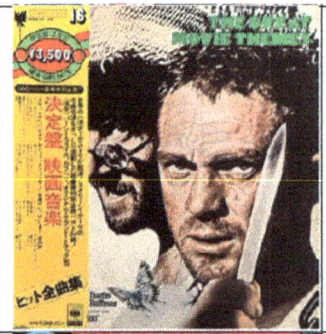

Title: The Great Movie Themes
Year: 1975
Country: Japan
Label: CBS-Sony
LP 1, A: 6 Tracks. **B**: 6 Tracks
LP 2, A: 6 Tracks. **B**: 6 Tracks
Info: A compilation album which includes music from; The Entertainer, The Godfather, Enter the Dragon and others. Box set of 2 LPs. Comes with an OBI and 1 insert.

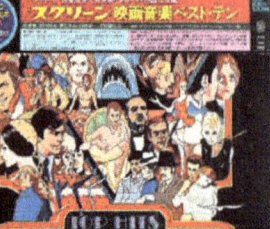

Title: Top Hits Screen Music 30
Year: 1975
Country: Japan
Label: CBS-Sony
LP 1, A: 8 Tracks. **B**: 7 Tracks
LP 2, A: 8 Tracks. **B**: 7 Tracks
Info: A compilation album which includes music from; Enter the Dragon, East of Eden, Melody Fair, Moon River, The Godfather, Jaws, The Way We Were and others. 2 x LPs, Gatefold. Comes with a horizontal OBI and 1 booklet insert.

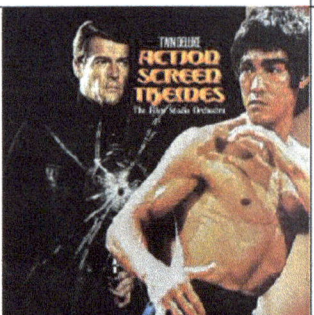

Title: Twin Deluxe, Action Screen Themes
Year: 1975
Country: Japan
Label: Victor
LP 1, A: 6 Tracks. **B**: 6 Tracks
LP 2, A: 6 Tracks. **B**: 6 Tracks
Info: A compilation album which includes music from; The Big Boss, Fist of Fury, The Way of the Dragon, Enter the Dragon, The One-Armed Boxer, Jaws, Zorro, The Exorcist, and 6 James Bond themes. 2 x LPs, Gatefold. Comes with an OBI and no insert.

Title: World of Bruce Lee
Year: 1975
Country: Japan
Label: Tam
LP 1, A: 6 Tracks. **B**: 6 Tracks
LP 2, A: 5 Tracks. **B**: 5 Tracks
Info: A compilation of music and soundtrack taken from Bruce Lee movies, The Big Boss, Fist of Fury and Enter the Dragon. 2 x LPs, Gatefold, and comes with an OBI and 1 insert.

Title: The Way Of The Dragon) - Joseph Koo
Year: 1975
Country: Japan
Label: Tam
Side A: 5 Tracks
Side B: 5 Tracks
Info: The Way of the Dragon original soundtrack by Joseph Koo. Includes a reproduction Way of the Dragon Hong Kong movie poster.

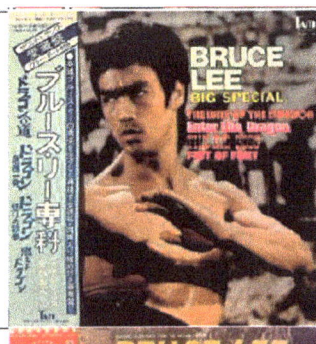	**Title**: Bruce Lee - Big Special **Year**: 1975 **Country**: Japan **Label**: Tam **Side A**: 6 Tracks **Side B**: 6 Tracks **Info**: Music from all of Bruce Lee's movies, except Game of Death. 2 x LPs, Gatefold. Includes an OBI and 1 insert which folds into 2 x Bruce Lee portraits.
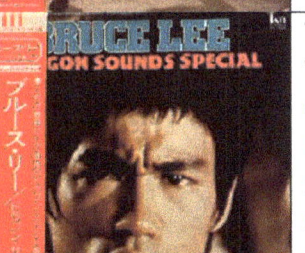	**Title**: Bruce Lee 'Enter The Dragon' **Year**: 1975 **Country**: Japan **Label**: Warner Brothers Records **Side A**: 8 Tracks **Side B**: 3 Tracks **Info**: Includes music from Lalo Schifrin and dialogue from Enter the Dragon. Comes with an OBI and 2 inserts.
 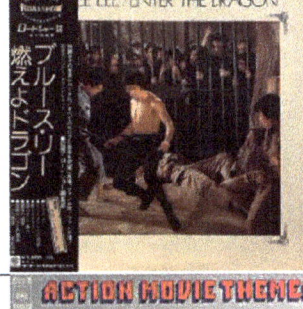	**Title**: Bruce Lee - Dragon Sounds Special **Year**: 1975 **Country**: Japan **Label**: Tam **Side A**: 7 Tracks **Side B**: 7 Tracks **Info**: A Bruce Lee compilation album, which includes music from the Tam releases. But this one also has Carl Douglas' Kung Fu Fighting. Includes an OBI and a Game of Death poster. There was a second release, but that came with no poster.
	**Title**: Bruce Lee - Enter The Dragon **Year**: 1975 **Country**: Japan **Label**: Warner Brothers Records **LP 1; A**: Dialogue. **B**: Dialogue **LP 2; A**: Dialogue. **B**: Dialogue **Info**: This record consists of dialogue from Enter the Dragon. 2 x LPs, Gatefold. Includes an OBI, 1 insert and 1 poster. The 1980 re-release had a green OBI and no poster.
	**Title**: Action Movie Themes **Year**: 1976 **Country**: Japan **Label**: CBS/Sony **LP 1, A**: 6 Tracks. **B**: 6 Tracks **LP 2, A**: 6 Tracks. **B**: 6 Tracks **Info**: A compilation album which includes music from; Enter the Dragon, The Great Escape, The Third Man, Bonnie and Clyde and others. 2 x LP, Gatefold with an OBI and no inserts.

Title: Enter the Dragon
Year: 1976
Country: Japan
Label: Philips
Side A: 6 Tracks
Side B: 6 Tracks
Info: This compilation album includes music from; Enter the Dragon, The Man with the Golden Gun, Bullet, Jaws, The Godfather and others. Comes with an OBI and no insert.

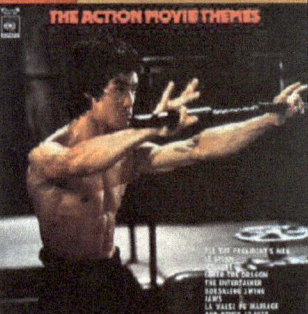

Title: The Action Movie Themes
Year: 1976
Country: Japan
Label: CBS-Sony
Side A: 10 Tracks
Side B: 10 Tracks
Info: A compilation album, which includes music from; Enter the Dragon, Jaws, The Return of the Pink Panther, Zorro and others. Includes an OBI and 1 insert.

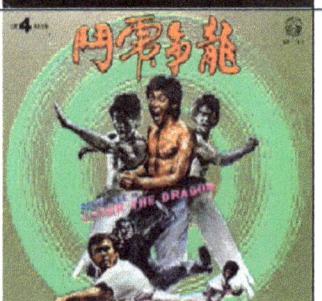

Title: Bruce Lee In Enter the Dragon
Year: 2076
Country: Hong Kong
Label: Stereo Records Company
Side A: 6 Tracks
Side B: 6 Tracks
Info: This re-release is not the Enter the Dragon soundtrack, but an LP of covers done by an Asian band called The Artchis.

Title: The Dragon Vs The Gunman
Year: 1977
Country: Japan
Label: RCA
LP 1, A: 5 Tracks. **B**: 5 Tracks
LP 2, A: 5 Tracks. **B**: 5 Tracks
Info: A compilation album, with music from; The Big Boss, Fist of Fury, The Way of the Dragon, Enter the Dragon, The Hills Run Red, The Good The Bad The Ugly and others. 2 x LPs, Gatefold. Includes an OBI and no insert.

Title: The Green Hornet - Still At Large
Year: 1977
Country: USA
Label: Nostalgia Lane
Side A: The Woman in the Case
Side B: The Soldier and his Dog
Info: Two Complete episodes of the Green Hornet Radio Show, which was first broadcast on Detroit's WXYZ Radio Channel in 1936.

Title: The Green Hornet
Year: 1977
Country: USA
Label: Golden Age
Side A: Justice Wears A Blindfold.
Side B: Murders and the Dope Racket
Info: Another two Complete episodes of the Green Hornet Radio Show, which was first broadcast on Detroit's WXYZ Radio Channel in 1936.

Title: American T.V. and Movie Songs
Year: 1978
Country: Japan
Label: RCA
LP 1, A: 8 Tracks. **B**: 7 Tracks
LP 2, A: 8 Tracks. **B**: 7 Tracks
Info: A compilation album which includes theme music from; The Green Hornet, The Untouchables, The Man from U,N.C.L.E. Bonanza, Batman and others. 2 x LPs, Gatefold. Includes an OBI and no insert.

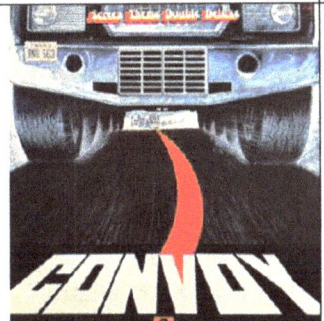 

Title: Convoy (Screen Theme Double Deluxe)
Year: 1978
Country: Japan
Label: Polydor
LP 1, A: 7 Tracks. **B**: 7 Tracks
LP 2, A: 7 Tracks. **B**: 7 Tracks
Info: A compilation album which includes theme music from; Game of Death, Convoy, Love Story, The Godfather and others. 2 x LPs, Gatefold. Comes with an OBI and 1 insert.

Title: Dragon Power: A Tribute to Bruce Lee
Year: 1978
Country: UK
Label: Satril
Side A: Part 1
Side B: Part 2
Info: A limited edition LP album by the J.K.D Band featuring the voice of Bruce Lee. This was released in association with Felix Dennis and Kung Fu Monthly poster magazine.

Title: Dragon Power: A Tribute to Bruce Lee
Year: 1978
Country: UK
Label: Satril
Side A: Part 1
Side B: Part 2
Info: The same as above album, but with a variant black sleeve cover.

Title: Legend of Bruce Lee
Year: 1978
Country: Japan
Label: CBS/Sony
Side A: 6 Tracks
Side B: 6 Tracks
Info: This has all the versions of Bruce's movies with 3 Game of Death tracks added. The 1st pressing came with an OBI and 6 colour portraits of Bruce from each of his movies.

Title: Screen Music Best Hits
Year: 1978
Country: Japan
Label: CBS/Sony
LP 1, A: 6 Tracks. **B**: 6 Tracks
LP 2, A: 6 Tracks. **B**: 6 Tracks
Info: A compilation album which includes theme music from; Enter the Dragon, Jaws 2, Emmanuelle, Convoy and many others. 2 x Vinyl, Gatefold. Included an OBI and no inserts.

Title: Star Wars - Saturday Night Fever - Convoy
Year: 1978
Country: Japan
Label: Polydor
Side A: 7 Tracks.
Side B: 7 Tracks
Info: A compilation album which includes theme music from; Game of Death, Star Wars, Saturday Night Fever, Bugsy Malone and others. Includes an OBI and 1 insert.

Title: The Best Collection of Movie Themes 17 -
Year: 1978
Country: Japan
Label: CBS-Sony
LP 1, A: 6 Tracks. **B**: 6 Tracks
LP 2, A: 6 Tracks. **B**: 6 Tracks
Info: A compilation album includes music from; Enter the Dragon, Game of Death, Shaft, The Great Escape, Convoy and 12 James Bond themes. 2 x LPs, Gatefold. No insert.

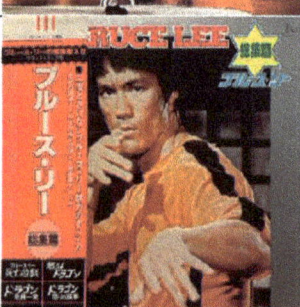

Title: Bruce Lee Complete Collection
Year: 1978
Country: Japan
Label: Tam
Side A: 7 Tracks
Side B: 7 Tracks
Info: This album included many Tam released music from all of Bruce's movies. Also included The King of Kung Fu by Kandy. Includes an OBI and 1 insert.

	**Title**: Bruce Lee's Game Of Death **Year**: 1978 **Country**: Japan **Label**: Tam **Side A**: 5 Tracks **Side B**: 6 Tracks **Info**: Original soundtrack from Game of Death by John Barry. Includes an OBI 2 inserts, and 1 Game of Death poster.
	**Title**: Tower of Death **Year**: 1981 **Country**: Japan **Label**: Victor **Side A**: 5 Tracks **Side B**: 5 Tracks **Info**: The official soundtrack for Game of Death 2: Tower of Death as composed by Kirth Morrison. Comes with an OBI and 1 insert.
	**Title**: Bruce Lee in Fist of Fury **Year**: 1981 **Country**: Japan **Label**: Victor **Side A**: 6 Tracks **Side B**: 4 Tracks **Info**: This album was a re-release of the 1974 Fist of Fury album. All the other original soundtrack releases had the same sleeve, apart from this one. This is why this is included. All of the re-releases had a different OBI and no inserts.
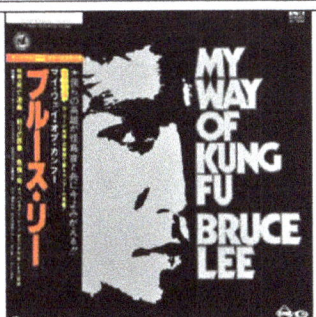	**Title**: Bruce Lee My Way of Kung Fu **Year**: 1979 **Country**: Japan **Label**: Victor **Side A**: 6 Tracks **Side B**: 6 Tracks **Info**: Contains Bruce's philosophy in English and Cantonese, and music from all of Bruce Lee's movies. Includes a Fist of Fury Hong Kong movie poster, an OBI and 1 insert. Re-released in 1981 with the OBI in red and no poster.
	**Title**: Screen Music Best 30 **Year**: 1982 **Country**: Japan **Label**: Polydor **LP 1, A**: 8 Tracks. **B**: 7 Tracks **LP 2, A**: 8 Tracks. **B**: 7 Tracks **Info**: A compilation album which includes music from; Enter the Dragon, Star Wars, Superman, Rocky, Bond, Jaws, and many others. 2 x Vinyl, Gatefold. No OBI or insert.

サントラより **本命盤** 肉声・怪鳥音入り

Title: Return of the Dragon
Year: 1983
Country: Japan
Label: Canyon
Side A: 5 Tracks
Side B: 6 Tracks
Info: Released to coincide with the re-release of the Big Boss and Fist of Fury in 1983. Performed by the Super Dragon Band. Includes an OBI and 1 insert.

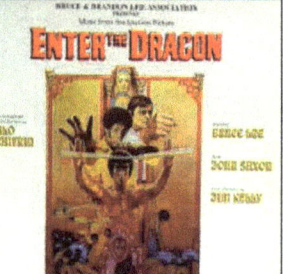

Title: Enter the Dragon
Year: 1998
Country: UK
Label: Unofficial Release
Side A: 5 Tracks
Side B: 5 Tracks
Info: An Unofficial Release. Produced by the Bruce Lee and Brandon Lee Association to celebrate the 25th Anniversary release of Enter the Dragon. No OBI or inserts.

Title: Enter the Dragon
Year: 2018
Country: UK
Label: Warner Brothers Records
Side A: 5 Tracks
Side B: 5 Tracks
Info: A limited edition picture disc album to celebrate the 45th Anniversary soundtrack of Enter the Dragon. Released for Record Store Day in 2018.

Title: Bruce Lee: The Big Boss
Year: 2020
Country: Germany
Label: All Score Media
Side A: 10 Tracks
Side B: 10 Tracks
Info: Soundtrack of the Big Boss by Peter Thomas (Revised Version). There were a number of different releases for this LP, including a limited edition red vinyl of only 400 released worldwide. This is the standard black vinyl. No OBI or inserts.

サントラより **本命盤** 肉声・怪鳥音入り

BRUCE LE
ENTER THE CLONES OF BRUCE
Interview with Frank Djeng By Rick Baker & Simon Pritchard

USA TOUR

Following the success of the Enter the Clones of Bruce US tour, we have caught up with Frank Djeng to discuss the Bruce Le events in L.A., San Francisco, Austin and New York.

RB: So, after six years it finally came to the conclusion, the long-awaited interview with Bruce Le was in the can and the documentary was completed. This then led to Bruce to come to the U.S. and promote the documentary. Maybe you'd like to tell us how that came about?

FD: It took us basically six years to convince him to finally be interviewed. And then, of course, we thought it's gonna be over and done. We had our premiere back in Tribeca Film Festival in New York in 2023. We thought, okay, that's it, we can kind of move on. But Bruce was still communicating with us regularly, well, with me mainly, and we were planning our festival run for the documentary. David (Gregory) thought, well, wouldn't that be great if we bring one of the clones to the U.S.?

And because Bruce Le ends up being the most enthusiastic person of our film, which of course was a surprise to us, since he was the one that really kind of held his distance towards us for so long. So, we thought, why don't we bring Bruce Le over to promote the documentary? We'll show the documentary at Alamo Drafthouse theatre and then will do a Q&A and all that stuff.

So initially we wanted to do that around September / October of last year (2023). This was back in July or

August. Bruce agreed and when he went to try to get the visa, he was told there's at least a three-or four-month wait to get it due to the backlog.

We knew then that that's not gonna happen. We can't do it in time. So we put the idea back on the shelf, so to speak. David thought, we should try again for spring because Alamo does their fantastic film festival twice a year, one time in the fall and one time in spring but to our surprise, Bruce got his visa in three days this time.

RB: Bruce took six years of 'humming and harring', what was the reason but then something changed his mind and brought him on board. What was those two elements?

FD: Bruce actually told us why during the tour. He said there were so many people that, he felt, tried to take advantage of him. When we first approached him back in 2017 at the Hong Kong Film Mart--Vivian and I, my wife who's also a producer on the documentary--he thought we were once again another one of those conmen who try to scam him of money, or that we have nefarious purposes. But back then he didn't say no. He never said no to our request for the interview. He's always said "later". The only thing he kept saying was "later". It wasn't until Tribeca accepted our film for its world premiere and David knew it's now or never. We must lock this film now. We must finalise the editing of this film, but we still don't have Bruce Le.

What David did was he sent Bruce a clip of what he would have included in the documentary had Bruce Le not participated and told him, this is your last chance to be part of it, because we've been continuing to ask him every few months since 2017.

I mean obviously COVID kind of stopped that for two years or so, but then after COVID subsided, again, we attempted to persuade him. So anyway, David sent him that clip. It was about five to six minutes. I guess that clip worked. That clip somehow changed his mind. I think that clip let him realize that we were not just serious about doing this, we've actually done it, but more importantly, we're not scammers. Within that clip, David also interviewed people who had collaborated with him. So, he realized, wow, you guys actually went to

France to interview Jean-Marie Pallardy, his former partner there, and then we have clips of his TV interview in France. So he knew this was a serious project and I think that changed his mind.

RB: I think the more you can give them questions that makes them think and it makes them show that you have a real deep-seated interest rather than just a journalistic approach helps. Do you think that helped when you spoke to him in Hong Kong?

FD: The thing is we sent him the questions not long after we met him at Film Mart. So, I don't think it was the questions that persuaded him. I mean, if he would have looked at the questions, he would have known that we were serious about this. It wasn't until he saw the clip that we had put together, in case he's not going to do it, that somehow changed his mind.

SP: Has Bruce Le ever been to the U.S. or L.A. before, and how did you adjust to the tour?

FD: Yes, but this was his first time coming back to the US in 40 years. He was invited by a local L.A. TV station called K.T.L.A., which is one of those syndicated T.V. stations there, for some event called 'Kung Fu Week'. So Bruce came to L.A. in 1983 for a week. But after that, he's never been back to the States.

As this was the first time he's been in the US in 40 years, I felt that he had pretty much had a culture shock because when we started in L.A. I think it must have been a shock for him to see that not only there are fans, these films are selling out.--because we did three shows in L.A., and we almost sold them all out.

I think it took a while, but when he first was in L.A., he was still kind of shell shocked, but he soon realised this wave, or this thing is real, that people still love these films.

Bruce saw the fans are not just his age, we also have people from younger demographics that approach him and know his film and stuff. I think initially he thought "am I dreaming?" That was the impression that he gave me.

It wasn't until we went to San Francisco, which is the second stop that I think he realised this is really happening and that these films are still popular, and people still watch these films. People want to see these films in theatres and that there is a new generation of fans who had never experienced these films in a theatre and wanted to do it. I think by the time we got to Austin he was completely comfortable with the reception from fans, from the media and all that because he also had the media interviewing him and stuff.

Bruce also did media and PR events when we were on tour. There was this guy in New York who was interviewing him and was rather young, in his 20s or 30s. Bruce just asked him "how come you guys like these movies? You know, you weren't even born when I made these movies. You weren't even born when these movies were in the theatre". The media guy explained to him "because we missed the wave. We missed the Bruce Lee wave. We missed the Kung Fu craze in the 70s and early 80s". They never had a chance to experience these films in the theatre.

They grew up watching these films on T.V. or V.H.S. or D.V.D., or whatever. And so now it finally gave them a chance to experience how we experienced them when we were in our younger days. And so that's why, yeah, that's why these groups of demographics who grew up watching these films on T.V. or physical media are excited about seeing these in the theatre and that the films are now restored, remastered and everything.

RB: How did that go for the first night in L.A., as opposed to when you joined, and you could translate a lot more kung fu jargon better to the audience?

FD: People think that we do this full time, but no, we have, well, in my case, I have a full-time job working for the Government. So, I couldn't attend the first L.A. screening because that was on a weekday, and I had to cover a colleague at the office that week.

So anyway, that first day went well, but the thing is he arrived a few days before the first screening in L.A. on Friday. He arrived Tuesday night because he requested that he arrived a few days early to get over jet lag. Wednesday and Thursday, he was just relaxing. Friday, that was the first day of screening. And that's also the first day where he had media interviews, so we found someone who majored in film at USC (University of Southern California) to help with the translation on that first day.

Bruce did admit to me that he felt much more comfortable with me because, one, he knew me and we've been communicating since 2017 and two, I knew a lot about his films and his career. My translation catered more to what Bruce was really trying to convey. I was told that once I arrived and took over the translation duties, he was much more animated and more talkative because he knew that whatever he's going to say will be faithfully translated.

SP: So, after L.A., where was the next stop?

FD: We went to San Francisco, and I felt that Bruce had the best time there. I think he was at his most relaxed because for one reason, we only had one screening, so it was not as hectic as L.A. where we had three days of screenings.

By this time Bruce was also taking this all in and realised he still has a fan base, so he's also at his most comfortable. night at the Alamo screening we also surprised him with Chiu Chi-Ling. We did so much to try to surprise him because Chiu Chi-Ling worked with him, and they haven't seen each other in more than forty years.

Chiu Chi-Ling lives in the Bay Area, so he's kind of like my neighbour. He lives like 15 minutes away from me. So, we arranged to have Chiu Chi-Ling surprise him during the Q&A. The Alamo Drafthouse has some weird rules that once the movie starts, you cannot go inside the theatre, so we couldn't have Chiu Chi-Ling go into the theatre in the middle of the screening and sit there waiting for the movie to end to surprise him.

We had to keep Chiu Chi Ling at the bar. Each Alamo theatre has a bar. Poor Chiu had to wait for about 45 minutes until we're almost done with the Q&A and then we had the Alamo staff bring him in to surprise Bruce.

He was very, very surprised. He never knew that Chiu Chi Ling was in the Bay Area. So now they have been reconnected and Bruce's very happy about that.

SP: What were the common questions the audience were asking Bruce?

FD: The most common question has always been "why did you become a director yourself?" Bruce Le said, "I wanted to introduce my own style into my film", because in the earlier films he had to work with a director, he must work with the action director. Bruce had to do whatever input they may have, right? The director wants him to do this, so he must do that.

In a way, it's almost like he's like a parallel to Bruce Lee. Bruce Lee first worked initially with Lo Wai and then of course they had a falling out, which led to Bruce Lee going to make Way of the Dragon as both director and actor. It's the same situation with Bruce Le where he wanted to have creative freedom. He wanted to show his own style. He started as an actor and became an action choreographer and then finally a director. That was the most common question that people asked him.

RB: What was your favourite memory from the tour you can recollect?

FD: Yes, Bruce brought a pair of nunchucks with him to the U.S. because he wanted to demonstrate some nunchucks moves during the Q&A's. Bruce did the demonstrations in L.A. Then when we were travelling to San Francisco, upon checking in, his wife has bought quite a lot of stuff in L.A., so when they checked in the luggage at L.A., the luggage was overweight.

They had to rearrange stuff at the check in counter so they could keep to the weight limits required. And I guess somehow, during the rearrangement, Bruce took out the nunchucks from the luggage and put it in his carry-on luggage.

Then when they went through the X-ray, it got picked up. The airport police stopped him and asked him why he was carrying nunchucks on to the plane, which is a federal law violation. Bruce and his wife can speak and understand English quite well and I guess he was trying to explain to the Police he's an actor, he's here to do demonstrations, blah, blah, blah. I believe the Police already saw us going through together, so they knew that we were part of the group.

At that point everybody else had already passed security. So, we're just waiting for them, because they were last to go through security. Bruce gestured to me that he needed help. I went over and explained to the Police that he's an actor, he's here to do Q&A. We had to show them our documentary's poster, and pictures of him as an actor to prove we were telling the truth. So finally, the police said, okay, well, we'll let you go but we can't let you bring the nunchucks onboard.

They would have to go back to the airline counter and check it in, which means you have to go back all the way out; you have to go through security all over again. And we said, you know what, forget it because if we do that, we're going to miss the flight.

We ended up forfeiting the nunchucks at the airport. When we got to San Francisco, obviously we had to find a replacement. So, Michael (Worth) and I had to go and look for a pair of nunchucks.

The problem was most of the stores in San Francisco Chinatown sell toy nunchucks, the plastic ones for kids. And so, we were looking all around for them, and we were like, my God, when are we going to find some? But finally, we stumbled upon this weapon store in Chinatown where they were selling nunchucks. We were able to get him a replacement pair.

From then on, Bruce made sure he kept the nunchucks in his suitcase. That was actually quite hairy because he could have been arrested. But yeah, that was the most memorable thing on the trip, preventing Bruce from getting arrested and getting him a new pair of nunchucks!

SP: Did Bruce do any other demonstrations?
FD: Yes, of course. And to be honest, I think we were all surprised by how fit Bruce Le was. I don't know his exact age, but he's at least over 70 now. During the initial Q&A, I was the guinea pig for him to do the 'Bruce fingers' thing. I tell you, boy, when he hits me with his arm, his arm is rock solid. I'm telling you, man. The force.

He told me that he still works out every day. He tries to work out at least once a day, but sometimes he would do like twice a day. And he walks every day but when he's home in Beijing or Macau, he works out three times a day, still does.

Initially it was me being the guinea pig and then later Michael was glad to be his guinea pig for the rest of the tour. But yeah, every time he does that little "Bruce's Fingers" demonstration, man, his arm is strong.

SP: So, after San Francisco you went to Austin, Texas. You previously told Rick and I that, that was probably one of the best audiences and events you did. What happened in Austin?

FD: Austin was awesome! Yeah. The ironic thing was before we went to Austin, we were like, why would we go to Austin? But then we had to because Alamo headquarters is based in Austin. That's where Alamo started. But we had to go to Austin also because Tim League, Alamo's C.E.O. is there. Now, well, you know, as of this conversation (June 2024), Sony has bought Alamo. So, I'm not sure if Tim League

is still going to be with Alamo now.

But yeah, so Alamo Headquarters is in Austin, and their CEO Tim League is based there. They asked us to go so we had to include Austin in the itinerary. But once we got there, we were pleasantly surprised. For one thing, the food was so good. The Texas barbecue, my god, they are amazing. I mean, I would fly back there just for the barbecue. It's that good.

O.K., but the main thing was, first, the theatre that we showed the documentary in Austin screening for the entire tour. It can seat close to about 400 people. It was a huge theatre, and the audience there were very knowledgeable. They asked great questions afterwards.

For that screening's Q&A we had a moderator. That was the only time we had a moderator for the screening because in all other screenings, David, our director, served as the moderator and sometimes we let audiences ask questions. But in the case of Austin, they had a staff member there serve as a moderator. He was the one who asked all the questions.

After the screening, we went outside to the lobby and we had a little signing there and then afterwards, we walked outside to right where the entrance was, and people would still ask Bruce questions. Again, those audiences were mostly very young, but they asked some meaningful questions.

Bruce was asked about his life, his beliefs in the philosophy of Kung Fu, you know, his training and all that stuff. So again, that was a nice experience because we West Coasters tend to have this preconception about people in Texas. We always felt that maybe, Texans are a little bit, you know... but no, not Austin, there we felt like we're in another West coast or East coast city. It was really quite surprising, and I wouldn't mind going back there, you know just to visit and just to have those barbecues.

RB: Now with the success of the U.S. tour, I suppose a lot of people are reading this and just general feedback I've got myself is that, when you guys release the second boxset is there a possibility of a European leg of the tour with Bruce Le?

FD: Yes, we talked about that midway through the tour. It was actually in Austin, while we were having that great Texas barbecue that we brought up that subject. Michael and I thought, wouldn't that be great if we can do this in the U.K. too? Well, initially it was just for the U.K., because David's from the U.K. We're thinking about at least London, Birmingham and Manchester.

We were thinking, maybe we can also do this in the UK and that it is something we can manage. We first started talking about doing this only in the UK. And then it got expanded when we approached David about it. David just said, well, why not France and Germany too? Bruce was popular there. So we have now started earnestly talking about doing a possible European tour, hopefully.

So that was something that's in the planning stage. It all depends on how well Volume One sells to be honest with you. The documentary has not been an easy project at all. I'm not just talking about coordinating and getting the talents; I'm talking about cost and planning and everything. I mean, it's a very costly project, you know. David has mentioned to us that this was the most expensive documentary project he's ever done, and the tour itself was not exactly cheap either.

If Volume One does well, then we will have good enough of nancial backing to do this European tour, so that not only will

we be able to promote, sell Volume One--obviously we can sell the Volume One boxset while we're doing the tour, but also to promote Volume Two. We don't have a date yet for when Volume Two will come out. Our hope would be that once we knew exactly when we're going to release Volume Two, we'll announce it and at the same time announce a European tour so that we can go to Europe, the UK, France, and Germany.

We have some great special features planned for Volume Two. When Bruce Le was here in the U.S., we shot quite a lot of footage of him. There will be a mini documentary on the boxset on Volume Two of his experience in America. We're also planning some other rather special features.

SP: Have you thought about bringing any of the other clones along on tour? Or have they shown any interest?

FD: We haven't asked the other clones, to be honest. We just felt that Bruce Le — the general consensus among us was that he's our first choice. It has always been Bruce Le because he's the most popular and most prolific. And because, well, Bruce Li, of course, he left the industry after his wife passed away and went back to Pingtung in Taiwan back in the 80's. He has never left Pingtung, he's still there. He's kind of like a recluse and we really don't know how receptive he will be to doing the tour.

RB: I think Dragon Lee could be a possibility.

FD: That's definitely a possibility but we really need to talk to them all first. There are plans to talk to both Bruce Li and Dragon Lee about either working with them in the future or joining us on a future tour.

Although we still feel like for the next tour, we'll still probably bring Bruce Le because of the fact that he's so popular in Europe. He's much more popular in Europe than the other two clones.

RB: The sales are based on the special limited box set, the standard boxset and then you can just buy the documentary on its own, can't you?

FD: Correct. Yes, the documentary is already out in the U.K., back at the end of May, and it's coming out in June in the U.S., the individual release of the documentary alongside the GAME OF CLONES boxset of 16 Bruceploitation films. The documentary is also on iTunes.

SP: The final leg of the tour ended at the Alamo theatre in Staten Island, New York. That was the one place we didn't go when we were in New York. We would have liked to as it's got the Flying Guillotine display and all those original posters, what was your time like there?

FD: Well, Staten Island Grand is kind of far away from Manhattan, even though in terms of distance, it's not that far, maybe ten miles. But then to get there is another story, you must drive, or you take the ferry. If you take the Staten Island ferries, it operates 24 hours and free, but even then, once you get there, you still must get an Uber or taxi to get to the theatre.

The Flying Guillotine was the name of the bar and that's also where Bruce got his fist print cemented as part of the 'Fist of Legend ceremony'.

And so that was, yeah, that was the last, you know, last leg of the tour. And again, the audience were very enthusiastic. We also surprised him once again, you know, by bringing Bill Louie there as he worked with Bruce in "Bruce versus Bill".

He was rather surprised to see Bill Louie there and they had a nice reunion. They both did the Fist of Legend thing. And the audiences were great. That was a nice large theatre too, showing that documentary at Staten Island.

Afterwards, we had a very nice dinner celebrating the end of the tour. And then we all went back to the hotel and rested for the rest of the night because we're all so exhausted! But it was a nice conclusion to the tour.

SP: As well as working on the second Bruceploitation box set, is there anything else you're currently working on or got anything else in the pipeline you're doing?

FD: Well, we are trying to get a film project going with some of the clones involved. Michael has already written the script. Hopefully it will take off. And if it takes off, we will not only have at least two of the clones in it, but also some classic kung fu stars from the 1970s and 1980s.

SP: Lastly, thank you again for your time, is there anything else you would like to add.

FD: Once Bruce Le told us he got the visa, it's almost like, my God, we had to start really planning this. It was really happening. We had to book flights, the hotels, contact the media and all that stuff.

I must give kudos to the staff at Severin Films, especially Deanna and Nicole, who really helped us with planning the trips, planning the flights and everything else. This tour wouldn't have happened, and it wouldn't have been so successful without their impeccable planning.

RB: Thanks again Frank and speak soon.

By Rick Baker

THE RESURGENCE OF BRUCEPLOITATION

From Low Budget to Cult Classics in 4K

In the wake of Bruce Lee's untimely demise in 1973, a curious phenomenon emerged in the world of cinema: Bruceploitation. This peculiar genre, characterized by low-budget films featuring actors who bore a striking resemblance to the martial arts icon, became a cultural sensation in its own right. Now, decades later, we are witnessing a revival of these once-forgotten gems, as boutique labels re-master them in stunning 4K, introducing a new generation to the world of Bruceploitation.

The Birth of Bruceploitation: A Tribute or Exploitation?

Bruce Lee's sudden passing left a void in the hearts of fans worldwide. Eager to capitalize on his enduring popularity, filmmakers scrambled to produce films that tapped into the public's insatiable appetite for all things Bruce. Thus, Bruceploitation was born. These films, often hastily thrown together with shoestring budgets and dubious production values, sought to cash in on Lee's image and legacy. From look-alike actors donning yellow jumpsuits to shameless rip-offs of Lee's most iconic fight scenes, Bruceploitation movies ran the gamut from homage to outright exploitation.

The Rise of Cult Classics: From Trash to Treasure

Despite their humble origins, Bruceploitation films found a devoted audience among lovers of martial arts cinema. While critics derided them as cheap imitations, fans embraced their cheesy charm, revelling in their over-the-top action sequences and unintentionally hilarious dialogue. Over the years, these once-dismissed films have undergone a remarkable transformation, evolving from trash to treasure in the eyes of cine-philes. Thanks to the efforts of boutique labels like Criterion Collection and Arrow Video, Bruceploitation classics are being lovingly restored and re-mastered in stunning 4K resolution, breathing new life into these forgotten gems.

The Appeal of 4K Re-masters: Bringing Bruce Back in Stunning Detail
In an era dominated by high-definition streaming and ultra-high-definition televisions, the demand for 4K content has never been higher. For fans of Bruceploitation cinema, the release of these films in 4K represents a long-awaited opportunity to experience their favourite cult classics in unparalleled clarity and detail. From the vibrant colours of Bruce's iconic yellow jumpsuit to the intricacies of each bone-crunching fight scene, 4K re-masters elevate Bruceploitation films to a level of visual splendour that was previously unimaginable. For die-hard fans and newcomers alike, these re-mastered editions offer a chance to rediscover the magic

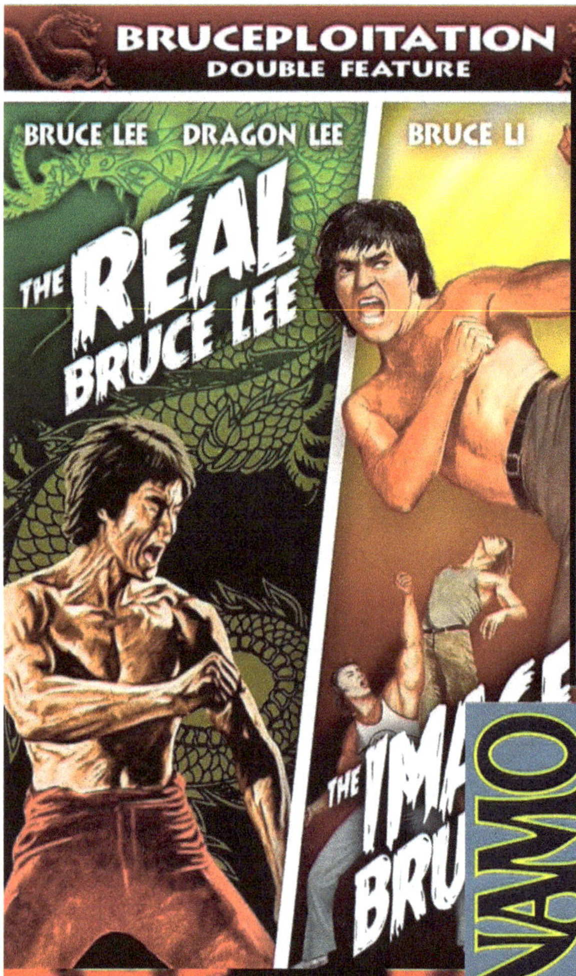

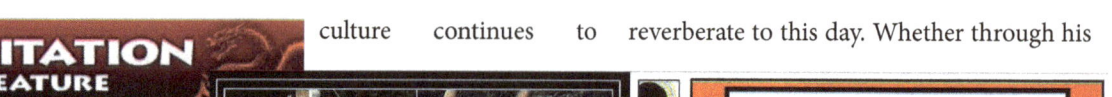

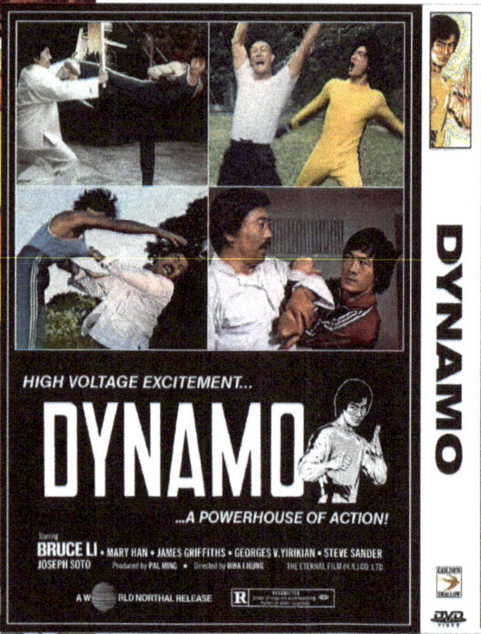

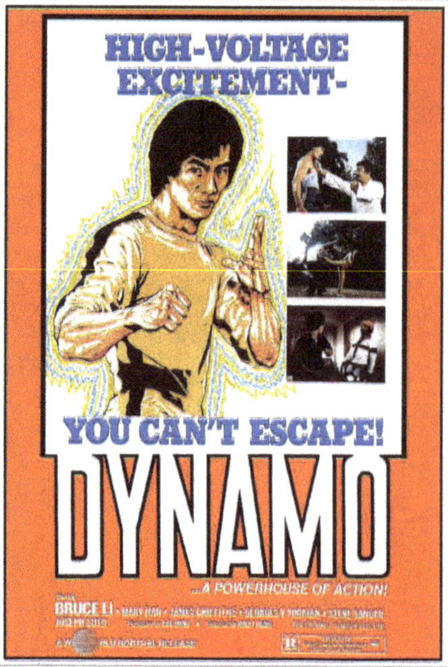

culture continues to reverberate to this day. Whether through his ground breaking martial arts films or the quirky cult classics that followed in their wake, Bruce Lee's influence remains as potent as ever. So, the next time you find yourself scrolling through your streaming service of choice and stumble upon a re-mastered Bruceploitation classic, don't dismiss it as mere schlock. Instead, embrace it as a testament to the enduring power of Bruce Lee's legacy and the indomitable spirit of those who dared to imitate him.

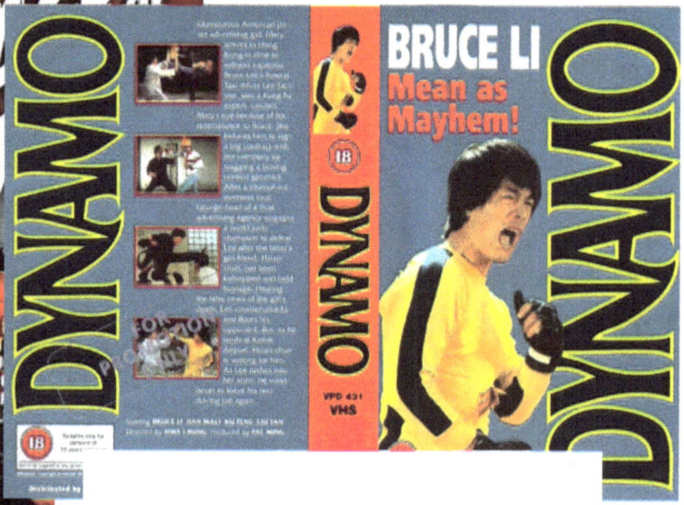

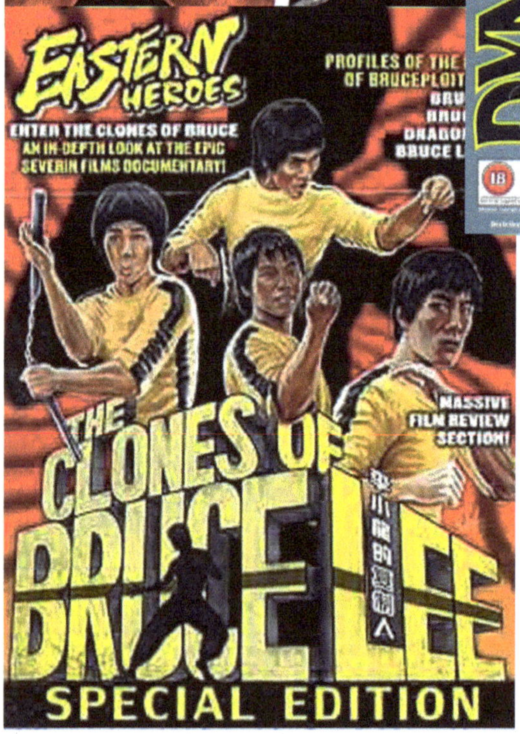

Conclusion: The Return of the Dragon in Glorious 4K

In a world hungry for nostalgia and craving the thrill of martial arts action, Bruceploitation films have found a new lease on life thanks to the magic of 4K re-mastering. What was once dismissed as cheap knockoffs now stands proudly as a testament to the enduring appeal of Bruce Lee and the creativity of those who sought to imitate him.

of Bruceploitation in a whole new light.

The Legacy Lives On: From Bruce Lee to Bruceploitation

In the end, the resurgence of Bruceploitation speaks to the enduring legacy of Bruce Lee himself. While the man may be gone, his impact on the world of cinema and popular

So, grab your popcorn, dim the lights, and prepare to be transported back to a time when Bruceploitation ruled the silver screen. With 4K re-masters breathing new life into these cult classics, the legend of Bruce Lee lives on in all its cheesy, action-packed glory.

LEGEND OF THE PAPER DRAGON!
NEWSPAPER THAT IS...

BY JASON MCNEIL

OK, CHILDREN. GATHER 'ROUND AND YOUR UNCLE JASON WILL TELL YOU A TALE OF TIMES LONG AGO. A TALE OF MARTIAL ARTS MAYHEM AND PULPY FICTION. A TALE OF SERIALIZED SENSATIONALISM AND BRUCE LEE DELIVERED DAILY TO YOUR DOORSTEP. A TALE OF.... WELL, LET'S NOT GET TOO FAR AHEAD OF OURSELVES. BEFORE WE GO ANY FURTHER, THERE ARE A FEW THINGS THAT YOU NEED TO KNOW ABOUT THE ERA NOW KNOWN AS "THE LATE 1900'S."

YOU SEE, KIDS, IN THE DAYS BEFORE THE INTER-WEBS, THERE WERE THESE THINGS CALLED "NEWSPAPERS." THEY WERE PHYSICAL MEDIA COLLECTIONS OF LOCAL, NATIONAL AND INTERNATIONAL NEWS STORIES, PRINTED ON CHEAP PAPER AND BOTH SOLD IN STORES AND - BELIEVE IT OR NOT - DELIVERED DIRECTLY TO SUBURBAN PEOPLE'S FRONT PORCHES AND MAILBOXES, OFTEN TWICE A DAY! MORE OFTEN THAN NOT, THIS HOME DELIVERY OF PHYSICAL MEDIA WAS PERFORMED BY ENTERPRISING CHILDREN ON BICYCLES - WHICH SORT OF RAISES THE QUESTION OF HOW THE NEWS INDUSTRY MANAGED TO SKIRT CHILD LABOUR LAWS... BUT THAT'S NEITHER HERE NOR THERE.

IN ADDITION TO NEWS, THESE NEWSPAPERS ALSO HAD SECTIONS DEVOTED EXCLUSIVELY TO DAILY, SERIALIZED COMIC STRIPS (WHICH ARE LIKE CARTOONS, EXCEPT THEY DON'T MOVE) AND FANS WOULD FLIP TO THE "COMICS SECTION" DAILY TO FOLLOW THE EXPLOITS OF CHARLIE BROWN AND SNOOPY, HEATHCLIFF THE CAT (WHO WAS MORE OR LESS GARFIELD'S "JOHN THE BAPTIST") AND EVEN ILLUSTRATED ADAPTIONS OF PULPY ADVENTURE HEROES: DICK TRACY, DOC SAVAGE AND, FOR AN ALL-TOO-BRIEF STRETCH IN THE EARLY 80S, COMIC STRIP FANS COULD THRILL TO THE ADVENTURES OF THE LITTLE DRAGON, BRUCE LEE.

YOU READ THAT RIGHT. FOR JUST SHY OF 13 MONTHS, IN 1982 - 83, THERE WAS A BRUCE LEE NEWSPAPER COMIC STRIP, AND IT IS WORTH YOUR WHILE, FANS OF THE DRAGON, TO READ THE REST OF THIS ARTICLE, ALONG WITH THE ACCOMPANYING ILLUSTRATIONS FROM THE SERIES, THEN DO A DEEP DIVE TO UNCOVER AND ENJOY THIS TOO-LONG HIDDEN GEM OF THE BRUCESPLOITATION LEGACY. FOR NOW, READ ON.

LAUNCHING THE LEGEND

IN 1977, AT THE HEIGHT OF POP CULTURE'S "KUNG FU FEVER," THE LOS ANGELES TIMES SYNDICATE APPROACHED COMICS LEGENDS MILTON CANIFF AND NOEL SICKLES ABOUT DOING A BRUCE LEE COMIC STRIP. THERE WAS MUCH DISCUSSION AND A FEW SAMPLES WERE DRAWN UP, BUT THE PROJECT ENDED UP NOT HAPPENING. REPORTEDLY, THE CREATIVE AND EDITORIAL TEAMS COULDN'T COME TO AN AGREEMENT ABOUT WHAT THE STRIP WAS SUPPOSED TO BE, SO CANIFF OPTED TO JUST WALK AWAY.

FIVE YEARS LATER, IN 1982, BRUCE LEE MANIA HAD COOLED DOWN A BIT, BUT THE LITTLE DRAGON WAS STILL A HOUSEHOLD NAME. ALSO, NEWSPAPERS WERE ENJOYING TREMENDOUS SUCCESS WITH COMIC STRIP ADAPTIONS OF THE BIG ACTION MOVIES OF THE DAY (MOST NOTABLY STAR WARS AND STAR TREK), SO SOMEONE AT LATS DECIDED IT WOULD BE THE PERFECT TIME TO REVISIT THE BRUCE LEE COMIC STRIP

IDEA. THIS TIME, THEY PITCHED IT TO WRITER SHARMAN DIVONO (WHO WAS ALSO WRITING THE AFOREMENTIONED STAR TREK STRIP AND WAS, IT BEARS MENTIONING, A PRACTICING MARTIAL ARTIST) AND ARTIST FRAN MATERA. (SUPPOSEDLY, DICK KULPA ALSO HELPED A BIT WITH THE DRAWING, ALBEIT UNCREDITED.)

THIS TIME, THE PLAN CAME TOGETHER, AND, ON 23 MAY 1982, THE LEGEND OF BRUCE LEE COMIC STRIP DEBUTED!

SADLY, IT RAN IN A RELATIVELY SMALL NUMBER OF NEWSPAPERS, NATIONWIDE, AND OF THOSE WHO DID INITIALLY INCLUDE THE LEGEND OF BRUCE LEE IN THEIR DAILY "COMICS SECTION," MANY, MOST AND FINALLY ALL OF THEM DROPPED IT IN FAIRLY SHORT ORDER. ONE OF THE FEW NEWSPAPERS THAT RAN THE STRIP FROM BEGINNING TO ITS ALL-TOO-SOON AND BITTER END WAS THE OLYMPIA OLYMPIAN, WHICH RAN THE FINAL DAILY STRIP ON 11 JUNE 1983.

IN THE LAST STRIP, ON THE LAST DAY, IN THE LAST PANEL, BRUCE LOOKS AT HIS NEMESIS AND SAYS, SIMPLY, "IT'S OVER!"

AND IT SO IT WAS.

YOUR RABBIT HOLE, SIR.....

THAT HAVING BEEN SAID, ITS ACTUALLY A PRETTY GOOD COMIC STRIP, AND WELL WORTH DIGGING UP FOR THE DIE HARD BRUCE LEE FANS OUT THERE. (WHICH, SINCE YOU'RE READING THIS, I'M JUST GOING TO ASSUME THAT YOU ARE.)

RANDOM SCANS OF THE LEGEND OF BRUCE LEE CAN BE FOUND FLOATING AROUND THOSE INTER-WEBS YOU KIDS LOVE SO MUCH, AND THE WEBSITE COMICARTFANS.COM HAS A NICELY ORGANIZED FULL WEB-PAGE OF A BUNCH OF ONES FROM 1982.

THE ENTIRE SERIES RUN WAS COLLECTED INTO TWO "24 PAGE MAGAZINE SIZED ISSUES" BY NOSTALGIA WORLD AND PUBLISHED IN 1983. COPIES OCCASIONALLY TURN UP ON EBAY, GENERALLY COSTING ABOUT $50 US FOR THE PAIR. THEY ARE WELL WORTH THE PRICE!

SO, DO YOURSELF A FAVOR, CHILDREN, AND TAKE A DEEP DIVE INTO THE PULPY PAST THAT IS THE LEGEND OF BRUCE LEE, AND HEARKEN BACK TO A TIME LONG GONE WHEN YOU COULD HAVE SOME NEIGHBORHOOD KID DELIVER THE LITTLE DRAGON

RIGHT TO YOUR DOORSTEP FOR LESS THAN 20 CENTS A DAY.

HAPPY READING, AND YOU'RE WELCOME.

ABOUT THE AUTHOR:

JASON McNEIL IS AN ACTOR, WRITER AND MARTIAL ARTIST WHO HAS APPEARED IN NUMEROUS MOVIES AND TELEVISION SHOWS, INCLUDING AS HOST OF STARS-STUNTS-ACTION! – TAKING YOU BEHIND THE SCENES OF ACTION MOVIES AND MARTIAL ARTS ENTERTAINMENT! YOU SHOULD DEFINITELY WATCH IT!

李小龍
BRUCE LEE
PHOTO GALLERY

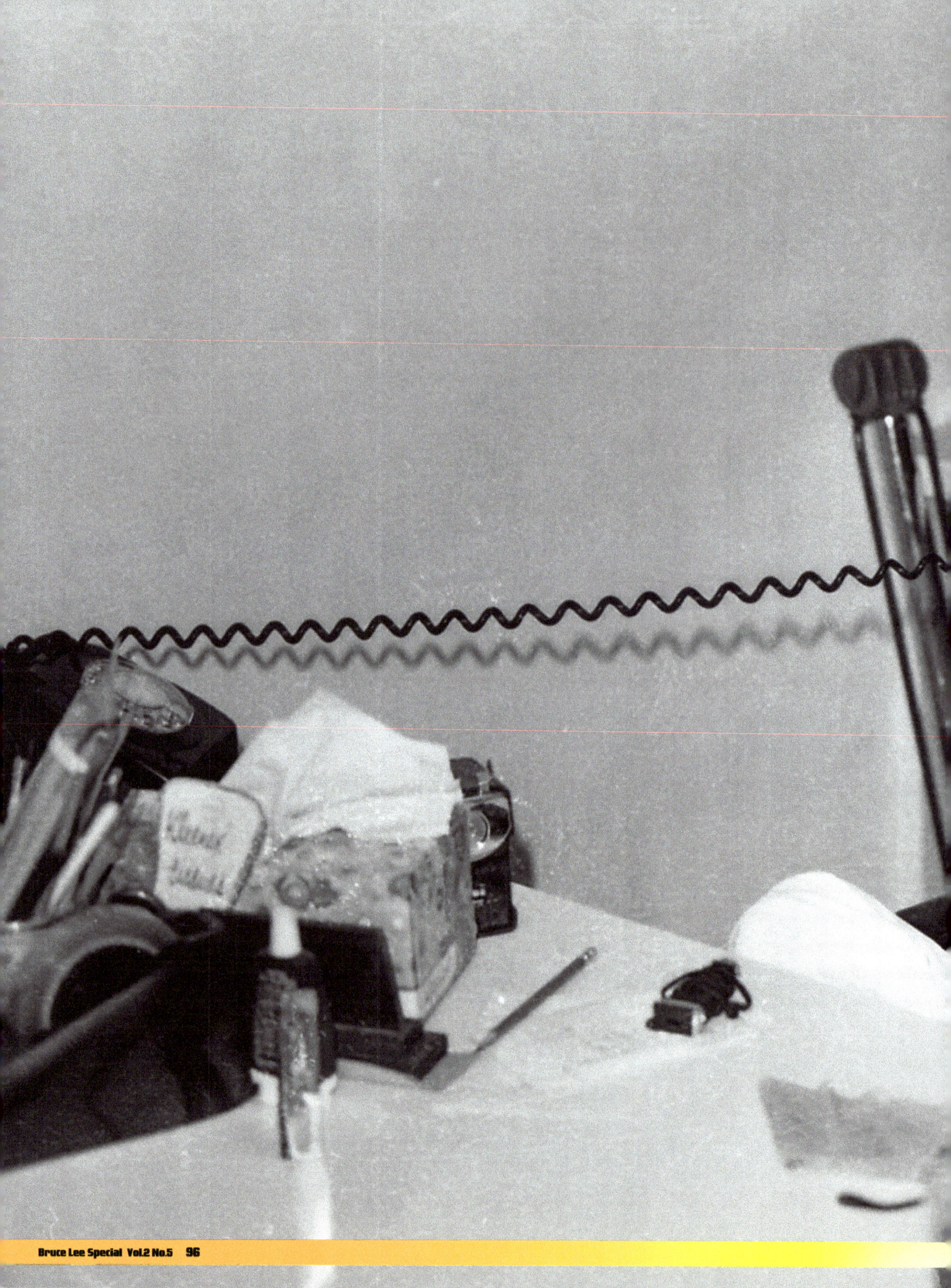

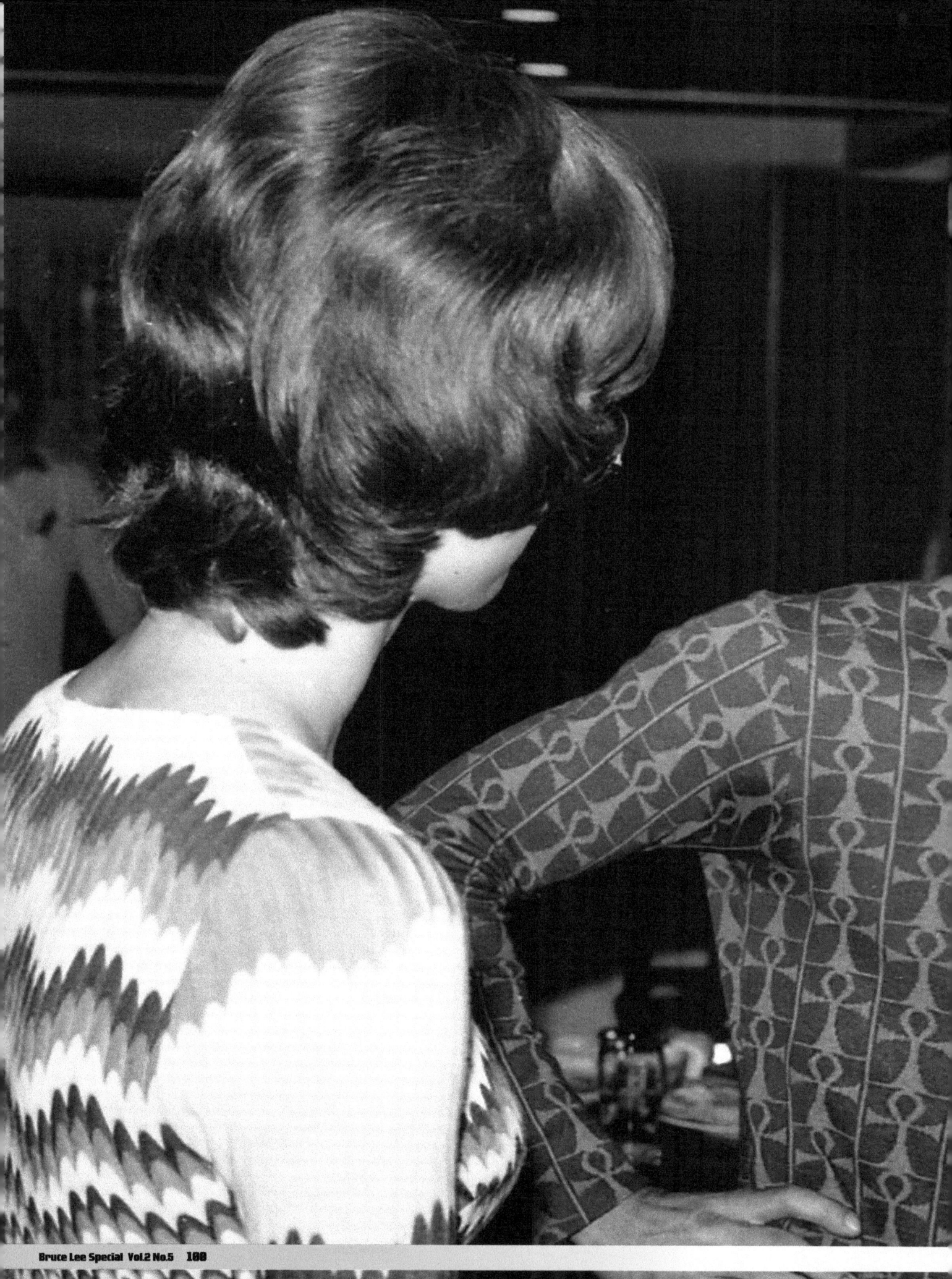

THE YELLOW JUMP SUIT

Movie References to Bruce Lee's Yellow Jumpsuit
By J.T. Williams

Bruce Lee's yellow jumpsuit from Game of Death has become an iconic piece of cinematic history. Even before his untimely death at the age of 32, Bruce Lee had already achieved legendary status as a martial artist and actor. Known for his profound influence on martial arts and cinema, Lee trained high-profile students like Chuck Norris, Kareem Abdul-Jabbar, and Steve McQueen. His role as Kato in the TV series Green Hornet, where he also made guest appearances on Batman, catapulted him into the public eye.

Bruce Lee's breakthrough as a leading man came with 1971's The Big Boss, followed by Fist of Fury and Way of the Dragon in 1972. The success of these films led Warner Brothers to produce Enter the Dragon, a film that remains one of the greatest martial arts movies ever made. Tragically, Lee passed away before its release. At the time of his death, he had already started working on Game of Death, a Hong Kong film he was also directing. In this movie, Lee's character ascends a pagoda, facing different challengers on each floor, including Kareem Abdul-Jabbar.

Production on Game of Death was halted for Enter the Dragon, and Lee intended to discuss a role with former Bond star George Lazenby for the film before his death. Given the existing footage of Game of Death, Golden Harvest hired Enter the Dragon director Robert Clouse to create a new movie around it. The resulting 1978 version of Game of Death used only about ten minutes of Lee's original footage, with lookalikes filling in for the rest. Despite mixed reviews, Lee's yellow and black jumpsuit became an iconic symbol.

This iconic jumpsuit has been referenced and honoured in numerous movies, TV shows, and video games. Here are a few of the more popular ones.

Kill Bill: Volume 1 (2003): Uma Thurman's character, The Bride, dons a yellow and black suit reminiscent of Lee's, which becomes blood-splattered during her battle with the Crazy 88. This homage by director Quentin Tarantino not only pays tribute to Lee's influence but also underscores the jumpsuit's association with martial arts prowess and cinematic legend. **Revenge of the Nerds (1984):** The character Toshiro wears a yellow jumpsuit as an homage to Lee's outfit. This reference highlights the jumpsuit's cultural penetration, reaching even into comedy and depicting it as a symbol of martial arts competence.

The Last Dragon (1985): The main character, Leroy Green, also known as Bruce Leroy, wears a yellow and black jumpsuit. The film, which itself is a homage to Bruce Lee's legacy, uses the jumpsuit to visually connect Leroy's journey with Lee's legendary status in martial arts. **High Risk (1995):** In this action movie, Jacky Cheung's character, a pampered movie star, wears a similar jumpsuit during the finale. This choice of costume serves to visually align the character with Lee's martial arts legend, blending humour and homage.

Shaolin Soccer (2001): A goalkeeper in this comedy film sports a jumpsuit that is a clear nod to Game of Death. The film, known for its humorous take on martial arts and soccer, uses the jumpsuit to invoke Lee's enduring influence on the genre. Additionally, "Bruceploitation" movies, which sought to capitalize on Lee's fame, featured lookalike actors wearing the trademark yellow jumpsuit. These films, produced in the wake of Lee's death, aimed to evoke his image and legacy, albeit often with less artistic success.

New Game of Death | aka Goodbye Bruce Lee: His Last Game of Death (1975) Bruce Li) plays a gymnast who film producers want to replace Bruce Lee for his role in Game Of Death after showing him a film-reel of what Bruce had completed Enter the Game of Death (1978) Mr Chang Bruce Le is hired by a Chinese espionage group to recover a secret document - crucial in winning victory - hidden on the top floor of a 6-storey ..

Dynamo (1978) Kung Fu idol Bruce Li plays Lee Ting Yi, A Hong Kong taxi driver whose striking resemblance to Bruce Lee catches the eye of one of his passengers who happens to be a movie producer. Lee is quickly thrust into the lime light and becomes a star but things grind to a halt when he is forced to fight in a fixed martial arts tournament. In video games, the influence of Lee's yellow jumpsuit continues to be felt. Titles such as Tekken and The Last of Us have included characters dressed in outfits inspired by Lee's iconic attire. These references serve to cement Lee's enduring impact on popular culture, with the yellow jumpsuit symbolizing

not just a piece of clothing, but a legacy of martial arts excellence and cinematic history. Bruce Lee's yellow jumpsuit from Game of Death has transcended its original context, becoming a powerful cultural symbol. Its recurring presence in various media highlights Bruce Lee's lasting impact on martial arts and popular culture, celebrating his contributions and preserving his memory through visual homage and respectful references.

The New Game of Death (Goodbye Bruce Lee: His Last Game of Death) (1975) The New Game of Death opens with Bruce Li playing himself (I think), picnicking with his fiancé and practicing martial arts. A film producer approaches him and asks him to help complete Bruce Lee's unfinished film The Game of Death. Enter the Game of Death (1978) World War 2 is approaching, and China is suspecting an invasion from Germany and Japan. Mr Chang Bruce Le is hired by a Chinese espionage group to recover a secret document - crucial in winning victor The legacy of Bruce Lee's yellow jumpsuit endures, symbolizing his lasting impact on martial arts and pop culture.

MARSHALL - GAME OF DEATH OUTFIT

dream believe achieve

Bruce Lee's Journey to Becoming a Global Martial Arts Superstar"
By Rick Baker

Bruce Lee's journey to stardom in Hong Kong and, ultimately, to global fame is a remarkable example of how positive thinking, discipline, and manifestation can shape a career. From the beginning, Lee knew he was destined for greatness, and his mind-set reflected that unwavering belief. In a Hollywood dominated by stereotypical roles and limitations for Asian actors, Lee faced numerous setbacks. Still, he remained focused on his goal, never letting rejection or stereotyping shake his vision. Instead, he developed unique practices to maintain his focus and channel his ambition, constantly visualising success and reinforcing his belief in his own potential.

In the 1960s, Lee was cast in small roles on American television, from guest appearances on shows like "*Ironside*" and "*Here Comes the Bride*" to a more prominent role as Kato in The Green Hornet. Though The Green Hornet gave him some recognition, it was short-lived, and Lee returned to a cycle of auditions and small roles. He continued to encounter racial bias and was often typecast as a minor side character.

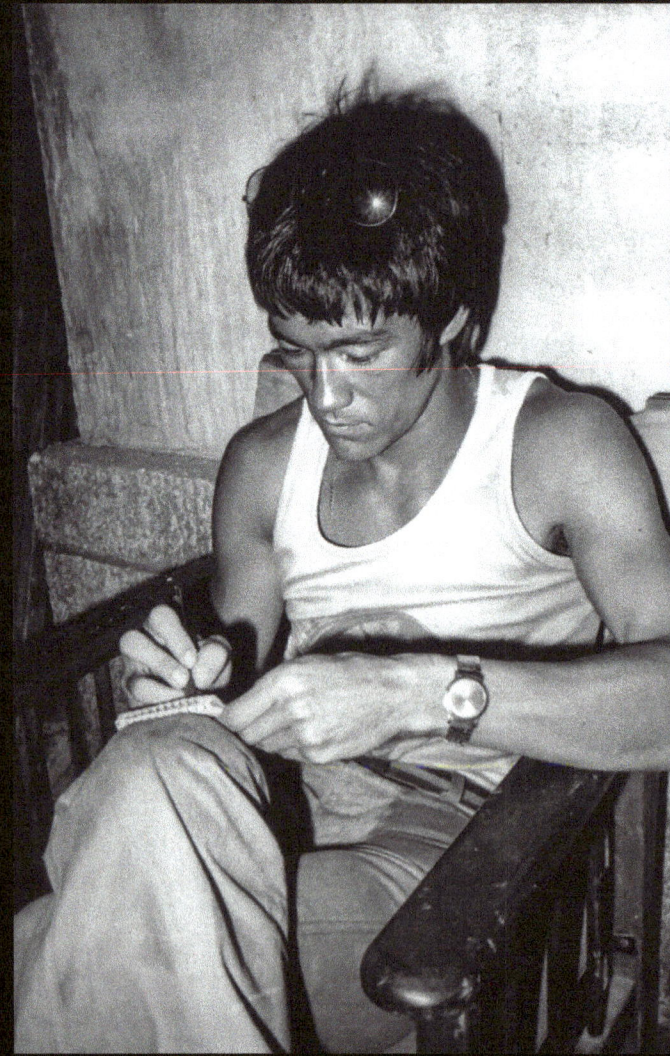

But Lee didn't let this dishearten him. He took the lack of substantial roles as a sign to continue honing his craft and strengthening his resolve, using visualisation as a way to keep his dreams alive. Each role he took on was another stepping stone, each audition a lesson. This resilience, he believed, would eventually bring him closer to his ultimate goals.

Part of Lee's unique approach to goal-setting was inspired by his study of martial arts, which, for him, was not merely physical but also spiritual and mental. He applied the principles of patience, balance, and inner strength from his martial arts training to his career aspirations. For Lee, mental conditioning was as important as physical training; he understood that his beliefs about himself and his future would shape his actions and, ultimately, his reality. This conviction was so strong that he practiced positive affirmations regularly, writing his goals down and revisiting them often.

One of Lee's famous practices was to write himself a cheque as a way to visualise future wealth. Lee wrote himself a check for a large

sum with a note specifying a time frame in which he intended to achieve that level of income. To him, this was not merely a symbolic gesture but a mental contract with himself. It was a daily reminder of what he was working toward and a physical representation of the wealth and success he knew he would achieve. Lee also kept a journal where he wrote down affirmations about his goals and dreams, often reading them aloud. His famous letter to himself in 1969 stated his intention to become "the first highest-paid Oriental superstar in the United States" by the early 1970s. This level of specificity in his affirmations showed the clarity of his vision and the strength of his belief.

When the opportunity with Golden Harvest arose, Lee saw it as the break he had been preparing for. Upon returning to Hong Kong, he was greeted with a surprising level of recognition, largely because of the syndication of The Green Hornet, which had been dubbed "The Kato Show" in Hong Kong, due to his standout role. Golden Harvest recognized his potential, and Lee was cast in The Big Boss, a role that became his breakout moment. Despite starting out as a supporting actor to James Tien, Lee's powerful presence on set led the directors to rewrite the script, making Lee the film's leading man. The Big Boss shattered Hong Kong box office records, making him an overnight sensation. Lee's determination to become the highest-paid Asian actor in Hong Kong was quickly coming to fruition, as the success of The Big Boss led to more opportunities and an increased salary for subsequent films.

Lee's rise to stardom continued with the release of Fist of Fury, which not only topped the success of The Big Boss but further solidified his reputation as a martial arts icon. Now with substantial creative control over his films, Lee's aspirations extended beyond financial gain. He sought to shift how Asian characters were portrayed on screen, crafting roles that showed strength, resilience, and dignity. His fame continued to soar, eventually catching Hollywood's attention once again, leading to his most iconic role in Enter the Dragon.

Bruce Lee's use of positive thinking and manifestation techniques remains a powerful example of the impact a strong, focused mind-set can have on success. He didn't just visualize his dreams—he embodied them, turning mental discipline into the physical manifestation of his goals. His story is an inspiration to those who face seemingly insurmountable odds, showing that belief, resilience, and clear intention can lead to extraordinary achievements. His life's journey from a struggling actor in America to a global superstar demonstrates the profound potential of combining mental strength with passionate pursuit, forever cementing his legacy as a pioneer in both martial arts and cinema.

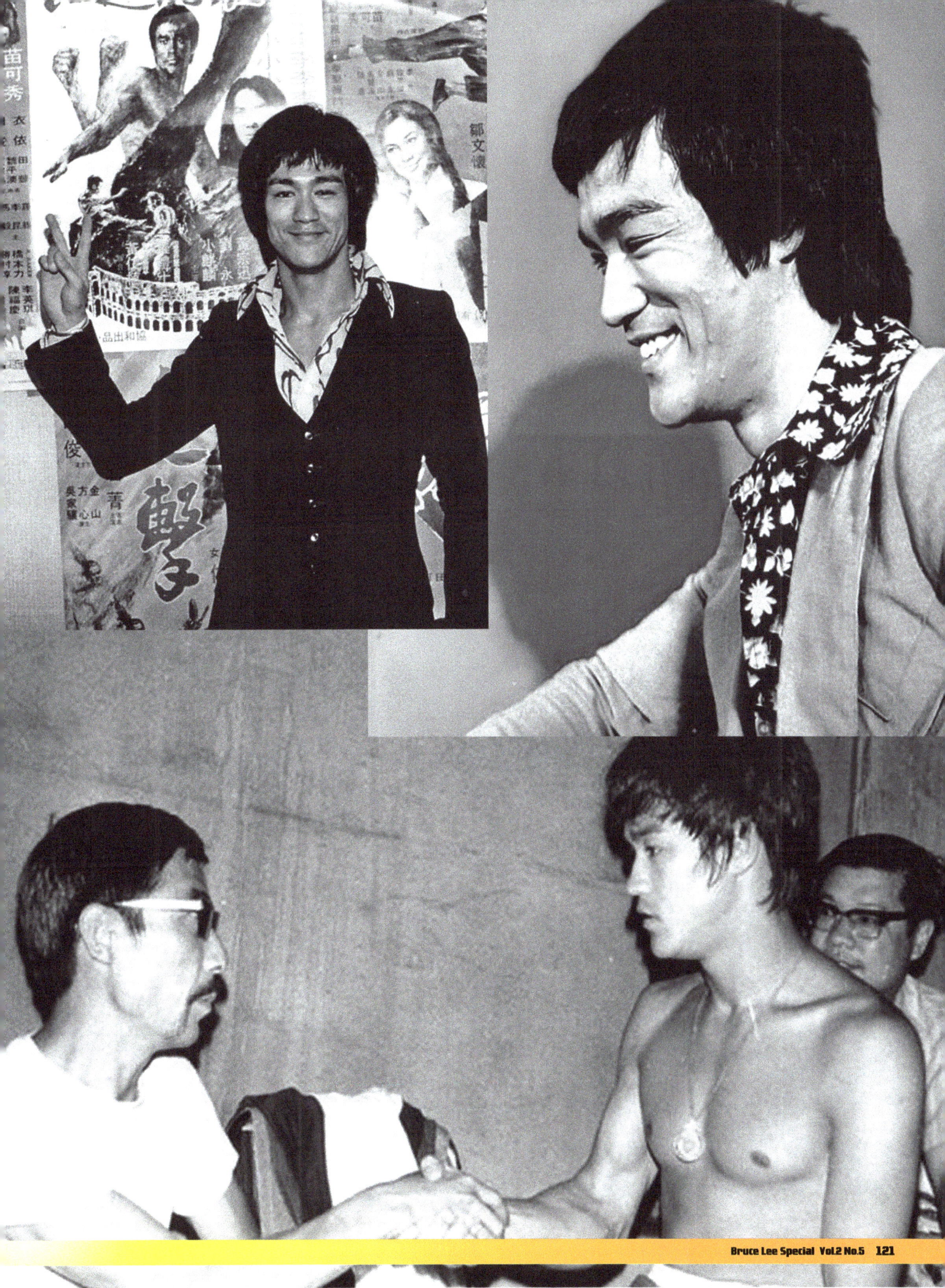

www.ingramcontent.com/pod-product-compliance
Lightning Source LLC
Chambersburg PA
CBHW061151010526
44118CB00026B/2942